Journal of the Librarian
Who Went to Prison for Money

by Glennor Shirley

DORRANCE
PUBLISHING CO
EST. 1920
PITTSBURGH, PENNSYLVANIA 15238

Dorrance Publishing Co
585 Alpha Drive
Suite 103
Pittsburgh, PA 15238
Visit our website at *www.dorrancebookstore.com*

ISBN: 978-1-6470-2220-4
eISBN: 978-1-6470-2966-1

Contents

Author's Note

"I kept going back to prison because I couldn't resist the money," I respond to those who question me about the years I spent behind bars in the Maryland prison system.

"You must write a book. When is the book coming out? You must share your story it is so interesting and compelling. Write a book!" Every conversation I have with friends or strangers ends up with the same three words.

Years after my final exit from the prison environment, I decided to toss the many prison information papers I accumulated during my twenty-plus years in prison. Going through the hand and typewritten notes from prisoners, in kaleidoscopic fragments, my thoughts and memory flashed to situations, encounters, characters, conversations, comments, educational topics, and humor that were my daily realities in the penal system. I had just read Michelle Alexander's 'The New Jim Crow: Mass Incarceration in the Age of Colorblindness[1] and it put in perspective my questions about the disproportionate number of black men in the United States prisons.

---

[1] Michelle Alexander's book: *The New Jim Crow: Mass Incarceration in the Age of Colorblindness.*

I ended up in the Maryland prison system because the lure of money in the system provided me with greater opportunities to live the American dream. As a new immigrant to the United States, my British Library Association degree, that in the Caribbean and the United Kingdom made me a professional chartered Librarian, was not American accredited. Consequently, professional library positions with a reasonable salary were out of reach. In addition to the money, prison became my learning ground for issues that were previously marginal to my experience. I learned about gay and transgender people, transvestites, racial inequalities, inconsistencies, and unequal justice in the judicial system.

These lessons made me aware of the privileges I had taken for granted in my native Jamaica with its population of over 92% persons of color, where upward mobility was based on education and social class, not the color of one's skin. Emphasis was on education as the sure means to move up the social, professional, and economic ladder. Less educated individuals in my country of birth, were often at the lower rung, working in various jobs as domestic helpers, nursemaids, gardeners, street vendors, and laborers. In the late 1970s advocates for social change demanded better working hours and a minimum wage for these workers resulting in the word "communism" being floated around. The outcome was 'political destabilization' led by the United States under President Regan resulting in mass migration among the middleclass families, described as 'brain drain.' In the United States, our adopted country, for the first time in our life we were confronted with racial issues, dubbed as "foreigners," and faced antagonism from groups who complained that the foreigners were taking away their jobs.

My first job as an hourly employee for a private contractor was to convert 5x3-inch catalog cards into machine readable format for computers. The cost of public transportation to get to work consumed most of my income. Thanks to my Jamaican friends, Marlene Lettman, Barbara Peart, and Ruby Tyson, who lent me money, provided shelter and offered mental support when I began to lose confidence in myself. They were the rock on which I stood.

My first job in a real Library was Library Associate in the Howard County System. To supplement my income, I worked evenings at (Maryland Reception-Diagnostic & Classification Center (MRDCC), a state institution where convicted felons awaited classification, a prison identification number, and transport to their assigned prison. Like those felons, my prison life began at the Reception Center. I served time there for approximately one year then transitioned to the Maryland Penitentiary, a maximum-security prison, for more money.

Determined to leave the library profession, I attended evening classes at Johns Hopkins University graduating with a Master's degree in Administration. Instead of leaving the library profession, however, I returned to Howard County Public Library as outreach librarian with responsibility to set up and operate a library at the county's detention center. The salary for this position was much less than in the state prison system, but I negotiated a flexible work schedule that enabled me to attend the University of Maryland where I graduated with a Master's degree in Library Science. I became Branch Manager in Howard and Baltimore County library systems before the offer of more money again landed me in prison as Library Coordinator with administrative responsibilities for all Maryland prison libraries.

Information requests in prisons took many routes. Face-to-face interactions. Letters via the institutional mail. Prison cohorts delivering requests to the librarian. Leaving written requests with a library clerk at either the magazine, reference, or circulation desks. I opened these letters, sorted them separating information requests from letters that expressed thanks for library services or expressing other sentiments.

This journal is mainly about my daily interactions with prisoners where I was exposed to the history, humor, humanity, kindness, dialogues of inspiration, aspirations, and hopes of the incarcerated men and women with whom I had daily contact. *Paroled! A Librarian Leaves Jail,*[2] an article I wrote for American Library Association Office of Literacy and Outreach Services, details some of my experiences. I have not used the correct names of prisoners and blocked out faces in photographs as I did not get their permission.

---

[2] "Paroled! A Librarian Leaves Jail," Glennor Shirley, Coordinator, Correctional Education Libraries. American Library Association. OLOS. http://olos.ala.org/columns/?p=107.

Chapter 1

The Reception Center, 1985

It is 5 P.M. I am anxiously waiting for the librarian who will replace me at the information desk. I must leave on time in order to begin my first evening job at Maryland Reception, Diagnostic and Classification Center (MRDCC), the temporary home for convicts awaiting classification for placement in a state prison. I see the librarian approaching, grab my purse, exit the library, and walk briskly towards my car to begin the commute to Baltimore, where MRDCC is located. Traffic to Baltimore is heavy. I have taken the wrong exit. I stop, ask officers sitting in a police vehicle for help. They tell me to move on because I had no right to stop my vehicle in that area. I rush to my car, wander around until I eventually find the street that leads me to MRDCC's entrance.

This is my first time going into an area where I will have direct contact with prisoners and am curious, full of wonder, anxiety, and fear as I stop in front of the heavy iron gate that bars visitors.

"Can I help you?" inquires a voice from the small cage-like window on the left.

I hold up my driver's license to the uniformed caged man, informing him that I am the new librarian. He scrutinizes the license, looks at me, then lifts the barrier, indicating I should proceed. I park, walk to the entrance to the building, press the buzzer several times before it swings open, displaying security guards, scanners, and people milling around.

"You the new librarian?" the security staff asks as he looks me up and down. He orders me to spread my arms so he can do a pat-down.

I'm not a prisoner, I am thinking, *but this sure feels like how I see them treat prisoners on television. I guess prison entrance and exit areas are the portals for beginning of power play in the prison environment.* I smile, trying to maintain a calm exterior. It does not take me long to realize that corrections officers at prison gates display power to ignore you as you wait, probe hands over your body like the beginning of sexual foreplay claiming to search for contraband, and keep you waiting until he or she is ready to open gates for entry or exit. Any display of impatience often results in open defensive hostility and the response "We follow institutional procedure and security guidelines." After going through several gates and an elevator, I find myself in the room where my direct supervisor, the library coordinator, is waiting. She explains security procedures and the library's relations with the Division of Corrections (DOC).

"Our education agency works in collaboration with DOC, the agency responsible for administration and security of the prisons, staff, and the prisoners," she says as she explains prison library services and security protocols. As she is talking, my eyes glance around at the tiny room, wondering how this could be described as a library. There is one cart with a legal dictionary, the *Annotated Code of Maryland,* some recreational reading materials, and request forms. Three shelves alongside the wall have books and reams of paper. Three boxes are in a corner on the floor.

I ask about space for prisoner visits. "In this institution prisoners stay for a maximum time of about six weeks. We are just providing them with some recreational reading and a few legal forms and materials to get them started. When they get assigned to their permanent institu-

2

tion, they will have a qualified full-time librarian and many more resources," she replies.

An hour later, Richard, the other part-time librarian, arrives. Like me, he has a full-time day job in a library and he wants to reduce his evening hours at MRDCC. I am here to fill the hours he is giving up. The coordinator instructs Richard to take me around the units for the first week, shares jokes with him, then says goodbye, telling me to contact her at headquarters if I have questions. Thus begins my prison life. Money being the motivation.

Reception Center Detainees

I accompany Richard to the housing units. The three-hour, twice-a-week library routine involves stocking the cart with recreational reading, legal materials and forms, informing officers before we enter each unit, processing requests, restocking the cart, book orders, and compiling monthly statistics.

As we enter each unit, prisoners are looking though the grilled areas of their locked cell doors, where they remain except on occasions when they are escorted to the administrative office for case management classification, medical issues, attorney visits, or for transfers to their assigned prison. In the lobby areas detainees watch television, play table games, or receive library services. An officer sits by the entrance, monitoring every movement.

My prison diplomacy begins the first day I enter the unit and hear the officer shout, "LIBARY." I cringe at this mispronunciation, thinking to myself, *LIBRARY,* but keep quiet as many corrections staff say the library is "too much of a privilege for criminals."

Majority of the prisoners at MRDCC are first-time offenders who try to use their street-smart mentality and joke around to show they are tough. Younger detainees constantly ask for "ghetto lit" books by Donald Goines and Iceberg Slim, the legendary Chicago pimp, or pass their time playing games and watching television. Older prisoners and repeat offenders often shake their heads, making comments about the immature behavior of the younger ones. A few older prisoners say they are encouraging and helping the "punks" to research their legal cases.

Repeat offenders make constant demands, often criticizing selections on the library cart. I soon learn that the criticism is more to show off their knowledge of the system and impress the younger detainees than because of real need for the information. Harrison, an older detainee and repeat offender, is one of the prisoners who tries to impress the younger ones. Each time I enter the unit, he comes up to the cart, asking in a loud voice, "You don't have *Black's Law Dictionary*? I need it to do my legal case."

The day he approaches the cart and sees the dictionary, he says with an air of satisfaction, "I see you have the dictionary." He returns to his seat without using the dictionary then or after. **He still periodically comes up to the cart** to ask for materials that he knows are not in the collection.

The evening when I arrive at MRDCC and hear that Harrison has left for his assigned prison, I silently rejoice that I would no longer be dealing with him. Not quite. Years later, after I left and returned to the prison system as library coordinator in charge of all the Maryland State prison libraries, I made regular visits to the correctional libraries across the state. On three occasions after I returned to the Baltimore office headquarters, the building's security staff informs me that state marshals were looking for me. They left no message since they said they wanted to speak to me directly. By the third time, my anxiety level increased, especially since these visits were shortly after the September 11, 2001,

Islamic terrorist attacks in New York. I wondered if the visits were related to a former Muslim coworker whom I supervised at the public library and who had the same name as one of the men associated with the 9/11 bombings. My mind kept flashing back to a situation with this coworker after the Oklahoma City bombing of the Murrah Federal Building in 1995. Initially when people thought the Oklahoma bombers were Muslims, he said that he felt isolated and hurt as his library coworkers shunned and avoided him, especially when he went to his vehicle and knelt for midday prayers.

The day when I finally came face to face with the marshal, he handed me a summons to appear in court to defend a complaint from Harrison. From his prison, location in Cumberland, Harrison had filed court papers requesting my appearance in court to testify that Maryland Correctional Libraries are not law libraries so they do not provide certain legal materials. The cost of security personnel, and equipment to drive him over 100 miles either way, plus my time from work so I could appear in court to say, "Maryland Correctional Education Libraries are not law libraries," was high. It is understandable, therefore, why I displayed amusement rather than compassion when a story about Harrison circulated among the prisoners. The story? In the institution where he was housed, Harrison was sitting on a bench waiting for a case manager. He attempted to get up, was unable to do so, and appeared to be in lots of pain. Eventually they realized that his testicles were wedged between the wooden slats of the bench where he had been sitting. Officers had to help extricate him. I laughed then, and rehashing this memory still brings a smile to my face.

By the end of my third month at MRDCC, everything became routinized and uneventful. I did, however, find some notes in my journal, titled *"The IMP, the Transgendered, and Jeffery."*

The IMP

His long golden-brown hair hung below his ears. His ready smile and laughter gave the impression of a teenager who is perpetually in some kind of trouble. From his spot on the upper tier, he saw me enter the unit with the cart of books, and immediately moved away from the other prisoners towards the cart where he stood looking at me expectantly.

"Come on, trouble," I said.

He laughed. "How are you?" he asked. "You look nice."

"Thanks."

Instead of going towards the cart like the other detainees on his unit, he stood by the side nearer to me than to the books. This position blocked the direct view of the corrections officer. The look on his face gave the impression he was seeking library information.

"Red shoes, red belt, red blouse, and let me guess—red…?" He looked at me as if to make sure that I understood what lay behind his unsaid words. "You know what I am going to say, don't you?" he said, looking in my face.

"I'm not a mind reader," I replied in my library voice, "but the cart is here waiting for you to select a book."

"I have to stretch out the time so I can bullshit with you a little bit." He laughed.

Another prisoners asked a question. I turned to answer. The imp moved towards the cart as the officer shouted for him to move on.

"I'm asking her a question," he said with a sincere-sounding voice and a look that said, "Gimme a break"—slightly defiant, but not insolent. The officer became watchful. He had no way of knowing what the question was. Prisoners ask simple or complicated questions either on reading recommendations or pertaining to their cases.

The imp pretended to look for something from the cart, then looked up at me. "I'm right?"

"Select your book and move on," I replied.

"When I go downstairs you can tell me." He laughed. "Just say yes or no."

I ignored him, concentrating on a library-related question from another detainee.

"Eh?" He looked at me as he signed for a book.

I gave him a blank stare. He laughed with a look of delight. On the lower tier, he mingled among the other prisoners, but suddenly I saw his head poking out from the crowd.

"Are you going to tell me? Tell you what, when you push the cart through the door, before you go outside, just say yes or no."

I smiled a "you-are-crazy smile" and pushed my cart through the door.

"Well." He pushed his head above the others.

"Goodbye," I said. "See you next week."

The next time I visited the unit, he had left MRDCC for his permanent institution.

Jeffrey[3]

Jeffrey was a notorious Baltimore slumlord in the 1970s. He was President of the failed Old Court Savings and Loan and was incarcerated for theft and misappropriation of bank funds that the news reported was about 15 million dollars. In addition to the public's anger at the fraudulence, there were derisive comments about him and his wife, Karol. People talked about their gluttony, describing them as "excessively piggish…" because they were very fat due to overeating. One news report stated that one evening, at a meal, Jeffrey and Karol ate over seven different desserts. Their 17 cars, not including what they

---

[3] *Jeffrey Levitt Stole $15 Million,* by Tony Kornheiser *Washington Post,* Sunday, October 26, 1986.

were driving, and a Rolls Royce golf cart with a TV and stereo deck on the dashboard were minor indications of the possessions they flaunted.

When Jeffrey arrived at MRDCC, correctional administration placed him in the isolated medical unit away from the other prisoners. He had access to lawyers and telephone calls in a way not available to any of the other prisoners. Prison administration justified this as a safety measure, especially from prisoners whose families may have suffered from his bank's failure. Prisoners were angry at the special privilege of this wealthy white man who, though incarcerated, the judge allowed $1,000.00 for weekly allowance that the news reported he overspent. I did not have much interaction with Jeffrey, as his lawyers and other visitors saw to his needs. However, curious to see if he was as corpulent as described in the media, one evening I stopped by the medical unit to ask if he required library services. No, he did not need library services from me. Yes, he was fat. In 1997, the *Baltimore Sun* reported that a freed Levitt lived in Florida, owner of a cigar shop.

Transgender or Transvestite?

In the Christian, class-stratified country of my heritage, no one openly admitted to being gay. Men who did not ooze machismo were often described as a "faggot," "funny," or even in more vulgar terms, and were sometimes victims of violence. Describing a man as funny was disparaging. It did not mean "humorous," but more like differing from the ordinary in a quaint, peculiar, perplexing way. My education on this lifestyle began the evening I pushed the library cart to the lower platform of the cellblock and waited for the officer to give the men permission to visit the cart. On the upper tier several men were leaning over the banister awaiting permission to come down. On the lower level a woman was among the prisoners seated at one of the tables. I assumed she was either a religious volunteer or a social worker, and was impressed by her apparent ease among the men. I wondered, however, why the corrections officer was not as vigilant about her safety as she was with the library cart and me. When it was time for the prisoners at the woman's table to visit the cart, she came up with them.

I guess she must be interested in the kinds of materials I have on the cart so she can counsel them for future discussions, I thought to myself as she stood by the cart with a strange exaggerated pose.

"You going to take a book, Pat?" the officer asked her.

"I looking at what they have for me," came a lispy effeminate voice from this body with its exaggerated swagger.

A sudden burst of laughter erupted from the upper tier. I looked up. The men were looking down, pointing in my direction, howling with laughter. My friends say I have a readable face, and I immediately realized that my face must have registered shock on realizing that instead of a female volunteer worker, I was looking at a male prisoner dressed as a woman. Embarrassed, I tried to act circumspect, resuming my professional library information provider face. It was too late. The men saw, understood, and could not stop laughing. I forced my thoughts and face back to the customer standing before me.

"Is there anything I can help you with?" I asked, trying to conceal my embarrassment.

He, who I had thought was a she, body gyrating, fingers strumming over the books, mumbled something and finally picked up a book, returning to the table with her companions. I tried hard not to stare and to stay in the moment as a library professional. My uncooperative thoughts were running a mile a minute to the next few days, when I would be telling my Jamaican librarian friends about this encounter. I completed the transactions, got ready to leave the unit, and could still see the amusement on the faces of those prisoners who had been watching me.

Chapter 2

Maryland Penitentiary, January 1987

Ruminating

After one year working evenings at MRDCC, I accepted the offer to work full time at the Maryland Penitentiary (The Pen), a maximum-security prison, located next door to MRDCC. This job meant I would now work fewer hours per week for a salary that was more than the combination of my full-time day and part-time evening jobs. Initially, nothing mattered except more money! A few days after I said yes; however, self-doubt and ruminating took over. Why would I leave my public library job, five minutes from home in an affluent community, for a job with a long daily commute to a maximum-security institution located in a high-crime neighborhood? This prison was home to those serving long sentences for committing horrific crimes. While the significance of the classification levels of prisons meant nothing to me at that time, I heard that the penitentiary was a more horrible and frightening place than medium, minimum, and pre-release prisons.

Am I making a mistake? Would this be so different from my public library experience dealing with all kinds of users? At MRDCC, I interacted with prisoners about two hours, two evenings per week with an officer next to me. Next morning I was mixing with regular patrons from the public library environment. How would I cope on a daily basis with prisoners who were murderers, rapists, drug dealers, and gang members? The media portrays prisoners and the prison environment with such negative sensationalism each time a crime is committed that I began to consider my safety and the nature and culture of prison.

"The money is good," I told myself. "And the system is not insisting that you get the American Library Association accredited library science degree. Most importantly, you will now have the evenings to spend with your son, who has Down syndrome, instead of leaving him by himself and worrying about his safety."

The night after I said yes, partly hopeful, partly concerned, I sat in my room thinking about some of my experiences at the public library I would be leaving. Trying to convince myself that all would be well.

"You are a brave and a strong woman," remarked my coworkers, marveling at my decision to go to prison full time. I laughed with outward nonchalance, hiding my inner turmoil as I pondered: *Is going to prison any more dangerous, or does it require more risk taking than accepting a job to drive a bookmobile in the United States shortly after I received my American driver's license and did not even own a car to do much driving on American roads?* In Jamaica we drive on the left side of the road and the steering wheel is on the right.

I reflected on my interview for the position of bookmobile librarian when I informed the interviewers that my library career started as a bookmobile librarian with Jamaica Library Service, but I had a driver and had never actually driven a bookmobile. The library director responded that for this position the librarian would be the bookmobile driver, a statement that did not fully sink in until the first morning I reported for work. There I saw a minivan with the library's name and logo and a man loading boxes onto the van.

It looks small enough for me to manage after a few days of getting familiar with the roads and the driving. Besides, I see a lot of women driving these things, so it can't be that difficult, I thought as I introduced myself as the new bookmobile librarian and asked the man if this bookmobile was difficult to drive.

He looked at me with amusement. "This is not the bookmobile. It is the library's delivery van. The bookmobile is located in Ellicott City," he replied.

"Terror" is the only word to describe my emotions the first time I saw the real bookmobile.

They expect me to drive this humongous monster? I wondered as I smiled at Bianca, the librarian who welcomed me.

The smile masked my fear as I tried to listen to her instructions. Her helpful and easygoing manner reduced some of my anxieties. We shared stories of our life as librarians. She oriented me to the community and driving in the United States and I shared stories about Jamaica Library Service. My first day on the bookmobile, Bianca drove, offering lots of tips, hints, and user information. The second day after driving some from distance, she stopped in the parking lot of a small shopping center and told me to take a turn. Nervous, fearful, but practical, I rose from the passenger's seat and sat behind the steering wheel. It was not as frightening as I had imagined. From high up where I sat I looked down on the cars, sure that since they were smaller they would keep away from this large vehicle. The directions on the 5x3 cards were not very clear, perhaps written for staff who were familiar with the county roads. Bianca realized this and made changes. I thanked her since I was not sure I would find my way with instructions that said: "*Look for a house with 2 white columns. Park by the mailbox nearby.*"

The third day, I expected we would operate like the previous days— each of us driving part of the way. Bianca, however, was on leave. I was really scared to drive by myself. The supervisor sent Dave, another librarian, to go with me. I assumed that Dave, like Bianca, would begin by driving part of the way.

"No," he said. "I have never driven the bookmobile. I am just here to sit with you since you are not familiar with the county roads."

My panicked mind shouted, *Are you crazy?* I did not want Dave or other library staff to have a negative opinion of me, so my now well-trained acting face took over. I explained my nervousness, unfamiliarity with new country, new rules, new modus operandi saying that driving on the right side of the road still made me uncomfortable. He was very understanding as I drove slowly, while he read the directions from the cards. We approached our first destination on Marriottsville Road, I slowed down, turning right up a steep narrow winding road with large overhanging trees on both sides. My silent prayer for no encounter with any oncoming vehicle up this road was answered. I arrived at the top without mishap. Patrons were very nice. The scenery, spectacular.

The return trip down the steep incline was more challenging. I didn't know how to properly position either the bookmobile or the mirror to see the road and traffic on the right in order to safely make a left turn. Fortunately, there was no vehicle behind pressuring me to move on. I tried backing up but could not get the unit lined up correctly. I explained my dilemma to Dave, who offered a solution. He got up from his seat, stood by the passenger door, bracing himself against the door, peered out as far as his neck could reach. He informed me when the road was clear. From my seat on the left, I looked for oncoming traffic on that side.

He said, "Make a quick turn now."

I swooshed the bookmobile to the left, stopped briefly for him to get back in his seat and put on his seatbelt. I breathed a sigh of relief as I drove towards the next stop. After that, whenever we were together, Dave and I would laugh about that day driving a bookmobile, and his nervousness at being my lookout man.

A few other bookmobile incidents stood out. Driving slightly downhill on a narrow section of Route 144 and taking more of the road than

I should, I panicked when I saw a huge truck approaching. Certain we would collide, I swerved to the right, hitting the brakes with all my strength. The loud sound that followed scared me into thinking that I had hit the mailbox on the right. I was relieved to see that I had missed it by about an inch. The noise I heard was the squeaking of the brakes and the protests of the books that hurled themselves on the floor.

The other incident due to my poor sense of direction resulted in my taking a wrong turn. Trying to rectify, the bookmobile instinctively found itself driving on the left side of the road as if I were in Jamaica. I thought the oncoming drivers on the left side heading for the bookmobile were either drunk or crazy. When they made no attempt to get out of my way, it suddenly hit me that I was the crazy one driving on the wrong side. Fortunately, there was a left turn, and before my large bookmobile and the oncoming vehicle kissed each other, I swerved left. Plunk, crash, swish. Sounds assaulted my ears. My heart was pounding since I thought I had hit something or someone, then I realized the sounds came from the books that hurtled themselves on the floor. I stopped, took deep breaths thinking that re-shelving was the minor issue. I was worried someone had contacted the police, or reported me to the library system. It took some time to calm down. Still shaken, I turned the bookmobile around and continued my journey, singing to myself to *Keep on the right side of the road.* I arrived late at the destination. The only patron, a senior citizen, climbed the steps, looked on the floor, then said, "Looks like you had a little accident, dearie."

Was going to a prison any more life threatening than driving a bookmobile on the wrong side of a busy road?

"It is unfortunate we cannot come close to matching your new salary," the library director wrote in response to my letter of resignation. The lure of money landed me in Maryland Penitentiary, a maximum-security prison.

Maryland Penitentiary

There are two ways to enter Maryland Penitentiary (The Pen). The side entrance on Madison Street next to MRDCC, or the ramp to the main entrance on Forest Street. Either way you stand in front of a grilled gate that blocks entry to those without permission to enter or personal identification. It is clear at these areas that power play begins with the officer who possesses keys to entrance and exits. The ease or speed of getting inside or out depends on the whim, efficiency, malevolence, personality, mood, or professionalism of the security staff who hold the keys. Inside the front entrance are benches and an overhead sign with visiting hours, rules, and the correctional codes. The wall to the left hold staff time cards and snack machines. The door on the right leads to the administrative offices. Directly in front of the entrance is a glass cage, a grilled gate, officers, guns, keys, and chains. Access beyond this point occurs only when an officer inserts a key through the blue painted grilled iron gate, where the overhead sign reads: *"All coats and jackets must be removed. All items from pockets must be placed on the metal detector."*

Through this gate you pass by the prisoners' visiting area, descend to the lower level to where the corrections staff offices and prisoners' cellblocks are located. Another level down, the gates lead outside to the recreation yard, grey concrete housing units, the prison workshop, and a formidable high fence in direct view of the guard tower. On the left side of the yard is South Wing housing for prisoners in isolation, on protective custody, death row, or those who are placed on segregation for institutional infractions. At the end of the recreation yard is the education building and the library on the left and the medical unit to the right.

I used this main entrance the day I interviewed for the library job but on my first work day I took the side entrance on Madison Street, where I had seen people going in and out. Above this gate is a little cage from which security staff grant access to those entering and exiting the prison.

I press the buzzer. A male officer stares down as I look up from behind the iron grill that bars my entrance, show my identification card, and inform him that I am the new librarian. I hear a click, push the heavy iron gate inward, and walk inside towards another caged area with towering walls on either side.

"Close the gate behind you," the officer shouts.

My first lesson in a real prison. Close one gate before you get access to another. I retreat, push and close the gate, feeling hemmed in as I move towards the second gate while asking myself what I am doing in this environment. About to rattle the next gate to draw attention for entry, I hear a click and see people on the inside pushing the gate towards me. I quickly step inside as they are exiting. Facing me are metal scanners, locked doors, more grilled gates, and an officer shouting at me, saying, "You can't take your pocketbook inside. You will have to leave it out here."

I look towards the lockers, where he is pointing not liking the idea of leaving my handbag in an area where so many people are moving around, not knowing who has keys to the lockers. I prefer to leave it in my car so retrace my steps to and from the car, following the previous admittance protocol until I am once again at the inner gate. The officer on duty searches my folder thoroughly and runs a battery-operated scanner over my body. I wait for him to open the gate and direct me to my next location. He ignores me, answers the telephone, addresses the three men who are shouting at him, talks to some of the medical staff, and reopens the gate through which I had just entered to allow entry to others. The power play of the key holder is clear. Finally, he looks in my direction and move towards the gate that would lead me to the prison yard, pointing to the right saying that the library is located in the education building. A cursory glance around the perimeter of the yard shows high walls with barbed wires on top. I am now inside the formidable grey concrete structure that I had passed at least twice each week for one year without much thought. Everything looks depressing. The yard is empty and quiet. I later learned that this period represents a shift change for officers and the period when prisoners remain in place for the "count" to ensure no one had escaped. Though anxious to get to my work area in order to look around before dealing with the prisoners, I consider this empty space as a kind of respite. I climb the steps to the education building, open the door and hold up my identification to the corrections officer at the entrance. He looks at me, scrutinizes my ID, then directs me to the second floor, where my supervisor, the education principal, has his office. The supervisor introduces me to the teaching staff, gives me a brief overview of the prison, the library, and the education department.

"The library has been closed for almost two years and lawsuits are pending about lack of library service. We need to have the library opened as soon as possible," he says as he hands me folders with rules, regulations, and procedures for every aspect of the daily routine for staff and prisoners.

"As a female employee in a male maximum-security prison, it is important to be aware of all aspect regarding safety. Prisoners are very manipulative. That is the nature of every prison. Female staff members are often victims of the prisoners' manipulative strategies. Your job and safety depend absolutely on complying with the institution's rules. The folders list the do's and don'ts of working in a prison. Please note especially the rules regarding not accepting or giving gifts to prisoners, mailing items for them, sharing personal information, and following the dress code by not dressing in a provocative way. It is important for you to understand that prisoners keep their eyes and ears alert and open, using any and every information to their advantage. Be careful when you are on the telephone, or speaking to other members of staff. No touching, hugging, kissing or signs of intimacy with any prisoner."

It didn't take me long to learn some of the unwritten codes, like how the prisoners engage in flattering staff, especially the females, to get on their good side. I experienced the warnings about flattery and compliments almost immediately after the library opened. In the beginning I would smile politely, saying thanks whenever prisoners complimented me. Later, I developed my own strategic response. One day several prisoners tried to engage me in conversation, signaling to onlookers that they have some control.

"You look real nice."

"I like your perfume."

"Nice dress."

Aware that other prisoners were watching and listening, I laughed responding loudly enough for all to hear.

"Thanks for the compliment, but in this place, if somebody puts a dress over a mop or a broomstick, you guys would say it looks nice."

Laughter erupted from among the watchers.

"Humor," I told myself then, "is one way to deal with these men who are extremely sensitive about being treated with disrespect. At the same time, I hope they get the message. I do not want to be distracted by compliments, real, or with intent to manipulate. My job is to provide information in a nonjudgmental way."

The correctional education classrooms on the second level have teaching, administrative, and security staff. Downstairs, where the library is located, however, the librarian and the security officer are the only staff members dealing with over a hundred users each day. That means my responsibility will include dealing every day with library workers who are incarcerated men as well as the prisoners who visit the library for various information needs. Unlike the officer on the second floor, who interacts only with teaching staff and students, the corrections officer on the library level sits at the entrance outside the library area as he deals with everyone entering or exiting the building.

"If you are unhappy with the performance and behavior of any of the men who work for you in the library you can fire them. We will go to case managers for more applicants. No worries, we have lots of prisoners applying for library positions," the supervisor says as he accompanies me to the library area, a large room with bright yellow empty shelves. A cursory glance in the area shows the circulation desk, a room with boxes piled almost to the ceiling, and the librarian's office. Glass barriers surround these areas, enabling all-round visibility. This transparency means that prisoners and staff would see what is happening in every area.

As we enter the library, I feel the intense, curious stare of the men standing by the circulation desk, waiting, looking, assessing. The supervisor introduces me to the men. Uncertain of the protocol since there is a no-touching rule, I keep my hands to my side, nod, say hello, and smile. These men, my potential library clerks, are neatly dressed in regular street clothing, a protocol that changed to prison garments with DOC written in bold letters after one prisoner walked out in a suit, and another left by mingling with outside service workers, hiding underneath their truck.

Chapter 3
Prison Culture and Language

Recognizing the importance of understanding basic prison culture, rules, and procedures, I ask the library clerks many questions, treating them like employees in a regular work environment. Later, as they developed some trust in me, they told me that they appreciated how I treated them with respect. My supervisor had said, "If you do not already know their crime, do not ask them, or search their records for the nature of their crime. Some of it can be scary and it may hamper your working relations with them."

I followed his advice, asking only questions that were related to library procedures, book collections, and the prisoners' activities that were based on institutional rules. Several days after my arrival, news spread that there was a new female librarian. This resulted in lots of written requests for information, and queries about library opening for regular visits.

The United States Supreme Court's mandate regarding prisoners' constitutional rights of "access to the courts"[4] did not stipulate method of access so each state in the USA applied different protocols for prisoners' access the courts. Law libraries. Public defender. Private lawyers. In Maryland, prison libraries are not access to the courts but the avail-

---

[4] Bounds v. Smith, 430 U.S. 817, 821 (1977).

ability of legal reference collections help to reduce prisoners' complaints and grievances regarding lack of access to legal information. This meant that the presence of a librarian resulted in all-round pressure for the library to be opened as soon as possible. A quick assessment showed that the most expedient way was to begin with partial service, building up a relevant collection as I become more familiar with the information needs of the users. I post fliers stating that the library would open in two months with partial services .

"This means," I say to the library clerks, "I need all the help you can give. You more than everyone else know the effects of no library services. Please share your skills and give me some recommendations. I need volunteers with skills in art to brighten up the walls, knowledge of legal information, typing, processing materials, etc." These prison clerks worked with me to get the library opened.

In the prison environment knowledge is power, so communicating to the general population that the library services would soon be available gave the library workers some power. I listen to and learn a lot from these workers, who willingly share institutional gossip including one that my predecessor resigned because of questionable relations with a soon-to-be released female prisoner from another institution. While I have no interest in pursuing the veracity of this, I used it as an educational lesson. Questionable relationships with prisoners could cost me my job.

Rules, procedures, regulations, dealing with prisoners, safety, manipulations, bureaucracy, and staff relations is a lot to take in during these first weeks. Listening to the prisoners, however, it is clear that they are very knowledgeable about institutional rules and procedures. Many of them had worked in various areas of the prison, gaining insight on staff, institution quirks, and loopholes. To them, every bit of knowledge was important, used when necessary to their advantage, to assist, hurt, extort, and bribe, depending on their motive and need to maintain superior status.

My commitment to get the library open soon brings dividends. Each day, needed supplies turn up in the library, independent of the necessary arduous process of going through the required bureaucratic and financial paperwork. One case that comes to mind is the time I was in need of typewriter ribbons for clerks to process the books. One morning one of the library clerks, with a smile, pulled a typewriter ribbon from his pocket and handed it to me. He and some of the other clerks who had worked with my predecessor had also helped to pack up the materials when the library closed. As he handed me the ribbon, I looked in his face, smiled, and said thanks. Did he expect me to ask how and from where he got it? I did not. I took the ribbon and passed it on to the clerk, who was processing the books. It did not taken me long to learn that in the prison subculture everything and every situation is potential for future bargaining. When he gave me the ribbon, however, it served as a warning for me to keep an eye on the library's inventory.

Why did I not ask questions when supplies showed up in the library? Was it naiveté, or the emergence of my inner cunning self? I prefer to think that it was my focus and intent on getting the library open to the general population. I express more thanks than suspicion, in front of everyone, to avoid the semblance of favoring one clerk over the other. The prisoners notice and often laugh, saying I had a devious mind, especially on those occasions when I outsmarted them, or they allowed me to think I had outsmarted them.

One morning, a nicely dressed, well-spoken male, with an air of authority, entered the library, welcomed me, said his name was Robert, he knew how desperate the prisoners were to have library services again, and he heard that I was in need of supplies. He offered to get some for me until I got my budget in order. I thanked this male member of staff for his thoughtful and kind offer. The library clerks howled with laughter when I mentioned this staff member who offered to get me supplies,

"Don't be fooled, Miss Shirley, that guy is just showing off. He is a prisoner just like us. He been in the prison system longer, know all the ropes, and the officers. He is one of those who suck up and do things for the police. In turn they turn a blind eye when he gives himself privilege." Another added, "We're not worried, though, 'cause some of us get things from him too."

Prison is where I truly understand my late father's warning, "Never judge a book by the cover." I had automatically assumed this individual was staff because of his appearance and well-spoken authoritative manner.

The clerks and I settle into a regular routine, focusing on opening the library. This period in my work life dispelled any myth that females were the primary sources of gossip. I listen to and overhear the frequent gossip and tidbits about staff, prisoners, relationships, and various aspects of prison life. These men became my greatest sources of information that include tips for my own safety. They warn me about officers who were in cahoots with prisoners and officers who "messed with drugs." Many of them say they knew some of the officers "from the hood."

"The only difference between some of them and we, Miss Shirley, is that we got caught. Look at the type of car some of them drive. They salary alone can't buy them expensive car."

At first I am skeptical, surprised at the comments, knowledge, and power the prisoners portray. I believe they are either trying to scare me or get on my good side in a manipulative way.

"They are subjected to institutional rule and probably hate the officers who do not allow them to get away with rule violations," I tell myself.

I retracted this thought after perusing literature on prisons and prison culture. I learned about the prisoners, their power, and the prison administration's accommodation to a certain degree. My readings also included information about corrupt officers who aid and abet prisoners, had sex with them, and also participated in drug deals. During my four years at The Pen, the behaviors of some officers proved that the prisoners were not making up the stories. I pledged to be cautious dealing with corrections officers and prisoners alike.

Prison Lingo

You Need a Rubber?

My first adjustment at The Pen was amending some my British English vocabulary and expressions. The transformation began the day my supervisor said to me with a look of amusement on his face.

"Glennor, please do not go around here asking the men for a rubber. Here in the U.S. we say eraser."

What did the clerks think on the occasions when I asked them where and how I could get a rubber? I figure it was they who told my supervisor about my rubber requests since they did not want to embarrass me after they realized what I was really seeking. My American friends erupt with laughter whenever I share this story. In America, a rubber is a condom, while in Jamaica, a rubber is the rubbery thing at the end of a pencil. We use it to rub out mistakes written with the pencil or pen. There is even greater laughter when I say that many Jamaicans call a condom "French letter," which according to the Urban Dictionary was the term used for a condom by European Theatre during WWII. It took me some time, but eventually I started saying ERASER without even thinking about it. Years later, on vacation in Jamaica at a friend's house, I had to correct something I had written.

"Do you have a rubber?" I asked her.

"Look on Tony's desk," she replied, pointing towards her husband's work room area.

Aware that I had just switched my language, I started laughing. She looked puzzled. We both laughed like teenagers when I told her what a rubber means in America. After that, we used every opportunity to say we wanted a rubber.

In Jamaica, "to knock up someone" generally meant we were tapping or knocking on their door to let them know we were outside, unlike in America, where it was a vulgar way to say someone got pregnant.

By the time I went to prison, I was saying napkin instead of serviette. This came about because of my experience in a fast-food restaurant. After asking the staff three times for a serviette and getting a blank stare as if I was from another planet, I got annoyed, and pointed to the stack of serviettes on the counter behind her.

"Oh, you mean a napkin," she said, handing me several.

In the land of my birth, napkins were put on a baby's behind or women used sanitary napkins during their menstrual cycles.

While they never became part of my vocabulary, I became aware of some of the prison lingo that helped me to understand what was going on around me. Some of these were:

> *Catch a ride:* Asking someone with drugs to help a prisoner get high.
> *Cell:* A prisoner's living space, consisting of a bed, a toilet bowl, and a basin (the days before cellphones.)
> *Cellie*: A cellmate. The person who shares the cell(living quarters) with another prisoner.
> *Dag-:* Anal sex.
> *Dis: Disrespect:* Someone's life could be in danger if a prisoner felt he was *dissed.*
> *Fence:* Someone buying and selling stolen goods.
> *Fishing pole*: String made from torn sheets, used to tie objects, mostly contraband and send through any opening,

when officers are out of sight. There have been a few situations where prisoners tore sheets to make ropes for escape.

Flip-flop: Homosexual acts.

Kite: Contraband letter. Notes among prisoners. Sometimes using a string, if they are sending it to another tier.

Moonshine: Making alcohol.

Mule: A prison staff member who illegally brings or takes out items for prisoners.

Sweet kid: Prisoner hanging with older prisoners, possibly for protection or...

Roadkill: Cigarette butts, picked up from the side of the road by prisoners who are allowed to work outside the prison. Re-rolled, sold, or smoked.

Shank: Knife made by prisoners.

Ticket: Written reprimand against a prisoner's negative behavior or for violating institution rules. This can cause a setback in a prisoner's release date.

Working at MRDCC did not prepare me for the job at The Penitentiary. The only commonalities were prisoners, correctional officers, rules and administrative protocols. As its name implied, the Reception Center was like a waiting room in a doctor's office. While you wait to see the doctor, you watch television or read and, in the 21st century, play with mobile devices. At MRDCC, the prisoners watch television, read, and play games as they await classification and transportation to their assigned institution. During this interim I had brief and marginal contact with them. Always under the direct scrutiny of a corrections officer who was a few feet away.

At The Pen, work involves daily interactions with hundreds of men—murderers, rapists, serial killers, child molesters, gang leaders, dope dealers—with one corrections officer seated outside the library entrance door.

Except for prisoners on segregation, protective custody, or on lockdown, the men followed a daily routine of hustling, bustling, and moving across the prison yard for a variety of predetermined activities under the watchful eyes of corrections officers. Their activities may include: working in the kitchen preparing meals for approximately 2,000 individuals, eating in the dining room at mealtime, work in the different trade shops, attend school, library, medical unit, specialized group meetings like veterans, musicians, religious, etc., play various sport activities in the big yard, and going to visiting areas to meet visitors, including attorneys and family members. Some prisoners choose to stay in their housing units watching TV, playing games, sleeping, reading or writing letters.

Prior to this job, like most Americans, prisoners were people I read about as headlines in the local newspapers, on radio, and on television. I never saw myself in any position with daily encounters that would become part of my work life. I focused on the paycheck while realizing that my big challenge in this arena of crime, rules, restrictions, and manipulations would be to maintain a placid expression.

"Aren't you scared?" my friends and family members asked.

"Most crimes take place in homes, on the streets, parking lots, malls, and in communities. In the prisons there are strict security measures and security officers twenty-four hours each day. The media sensationalize activities in the prisons, just like airplane and motor vehicle accidents. There are far more road traffic accidents resulting in many more deaths but the constant media repetition of the airline accidents makes them seem more scary." I often end my statement with a laugh. "The need for more money made me end up in prison just like the criminals."

Because the library was closed for a long period, there is almost no documentation to guide me. Instead of complaining, I consider it an opportunity to set up library service as I envision it. I know it is not going to be easy. I will be a one-person library manager responsible for all aspect of services for men of varying race, education, social, and mental levels. I have to develop a collection that is relevant to the varying needs of this diverse population. Areas like legal reference, materials to complement the educational curriculum for GED, and to prepare prisoners for reentering society are new to me. To educate myself, I visit academic, public, and special libraries to learn about relevant collections, and programs that meet the information needs, interactions among prisoners, librarians, and various prison staff members. These visits highlighted the differences among libraries, librarians, services, routines, attitudes, and the varying institutional administrative support. For me, the most surprising aspect was seeing the extent to which librarians and other staff members rely on prisoners who work in the various areas. This demonstrated how much clout incarcerated persons have and display in the prison environment.

Aware that I too would be depending on prisoners, I knew instinctively that I had to take charge from the onset, displaying neither fear nor weakness, but being assertive. I could sense the prisoners watching, analyzing, assessing, and testing me, as they mentally note my reactions to their evasive answers to some of my questions. Correctional officers were also observing me and my interactions with the prisoners. Through the prison grapevine I heard that there were comments alluding that I was a good-looking, stylishly dressed, obviously educated and bright woman so:

"Why would a women like her want to work in a prison? Is it that women like her couldn't get a better job, likes to be around men, had problems elsewhere and this is the only available job?"

My good fortune was that Row, the officer assigned to the library, was fair, firm, and well respected. He was not one of the "mules," the moniker for staff who violated institutional rules in the corrections environment. Row and I developed a good working relationship, agreeing on behaviors and security issues. He identified and warned me about the prisoners who were likely to cause problems and I shared my concerns about the questionable behaviors. He never used profanities in my presence, unlike many of the other officers, and the prisoners respected him.

Computers in the Prison Library

Computers were new and almost nonexistent in prison libraries when I entered the system. While funding was an issue, the greater obstacle was the correctional administration's sensitivity to negative comments from the public, including the media, who said prisoners' access to this technology was too much of a benefit. Once, on air I heard a television reporter making negative comments about the State considering providing computers to criminals while many schools in Baltimore City did not have computers.

The day I opened one of the boxes piled up in the work room and saw a Commodore 64 computer, I was thrilled since I had just purchased a similar computer for my home use. Fully aware now of the power of knowledge behind the walls, I promised to teach the library workers how to use this computer. At home each evening, I practiced on and read all I could about my newly purchased device. Next day I taught the clerks how to use Commodore 64[5] They were impressed with my expertise. The device was used only in the workroom and not available to the general library users, but using it earned library clerks

---

[5] https://www.washingtonpost.com/local/glennor-shirley-head-librarian-for-md-prisons-believes-in-books-behind-bars/2011/03/25/AFXcTbYB_story.html?utm_term=.36dbc36ee952.

more respect among the general population. When I sought and got DOC's permission to add computers for the general population, procedures were added to meet the DOC codes and rules. There was no access to the internet. When the nation's two major proprietary legal database providers developed online services, our system acquired legal database on CD-ROMS and, later, DVDs. At that time, according to a news report, Maryland was the only prison in the United States with this kind of computer access.

Towards the end of my first month at The Pen, I sensed a more relaxed, positive attitude change among the library clerks. They were more helpful, identified artists to help create signs and artwork, and cooperated fully in helping me to get the library ready for opening. During this initial period, the requests I received from prisoners on death row, segregation, and protective custody increased my awareness of the legal needs and helped me build a collection that was more relevant to their needs.

Protective Custody

Just when I thought that I had come to terms with all my questions regarding prison library services, the clerks warned me about the protective custody (PC) housing unit prisoners. These individuals were the most disliked group in the prison because they were child molesters, committed crimes against old people, and snitched on other prisoners. PC residents never mixed with the general population, remaining in their cells for their own safety. Each day they are allowed one hour outside their cell for recreation and commissary. To prevent fights or killings during this period, the rest of the population was locked in their cells. Officers and clerks warned that the demanding and complaining nature of PC prisoners resulted in many grievances and lawsuits against the library. This proved true as majority of the grievances against the library came from prisoners in PC units. One case stood out. I received a summons to appear in court because of a grievance against the library's censorship of materials sent to PC. The claim was that the library was removing scantily dressed, bikini-clad women from the magazines before sending them to the unit. At the hearing I explained to the administrative judge:

"We provide approximately 1,700 men with access to magazine and books that we purchase from a small budget. Each day, about 200 users visit the library to browse the few magazines. Our efforts at ensuring that users do not tear out pages is to hire well-respected prison clerks, and depend on them to alert us if they find that pages are missing. In the prison environment, however, this 'snitching' may put someone's life at risk. Like any public or academic libraries outside the prison community, we do not allow current magazines to be taken from the library. We hold a user's identification card and do a cursory search for missing pages when the magazine is returned. We circulate the older magazines to segregation units, including PC. The high usage and circulation makes it difficult to ensure that every page will be intact. While we are not a law library, nor are we access to the courts, we concentrate more on the security of legal materials so we can provide prisoners with information or materials that will assist them with their legal issues."

The judge dismissed the prisoner's complaint.

Access to the Courts

The United States Supreme Court *Bounds v. Smith*, 430 U.S. (1977), states prison authorities must "assist prisoners in the preparation and filing of meaningful legal papers by providing prisoners with adequate law libraries or adequate assistance from persons trained in the law." Across the United States, prison systems conform to this mandate in various ways. Establishing law libraries with specific legal titles. Jailhouse lawyers. Private lawyers. Public defenders. Providing funds to purchase legal materials in the libraries or elsewhere in the prison.

The Maryland the Division of Corrections Prisoners Handbook stated that prisoners may get help from their lawyers, a legal referral service or directory, clerks of court, and PRISM (Prisoner Rights Information System of Maryland, Inc.), a group of attorneys who contract with the Department of Public Safety and Correctional Services to provide legal services to prisoners with certain types of legal claims, state public defender's office, and trial judges for special cases. It also stated that institutional librarians may not give legal advice but could help prisoners in finding legal materials. For prisoners needing legal help but unable to afford a lawyer, the courts would provide a lawyer when the prisoner's legal action falls under the Uniform Post-Conviction Procedure Act of the Annotated Code of Maryland.

Library users complained constantly about the inaccessibility of the public defender. The library was their alternative resource. Some prisoners told me that they gave their public defender the information they researched in the prison library.

Prisons as Total Institutions

My research for information on prison environment led me to Erving Goffman, the Canadian sociologist. In *Characteristics of Total Institutions*,[6] Goffman described prisons as being: "Symbolized by the barrier to social intercourse with the outside that is often built right into the

---

[6] Erving Goffman, *Characteristics of Total Institutions*. http://www.markfoster.net/neurelitism/totalinstitutions.pdf.

physical plant: locked doors, high walls, barbed wire, cliffs and water, open terrain, and so forth."

He wrote that modern society's basic social arrangement is that individuals tend to sleep, play, and work in different places, each situation with a different set of authority figures and without an overall rational plan. He described total institutions as a breakdown of the kinds of barriers ordinarily separating the three spheres of life where every aspect of life is conducted in the same place and under the same single authority with each phase of daily activity being carried out in the immediate company of a large batch of others who are treated alike and required to do the same things together.

Goffman stated that every phase of daily activities is tightly scheduled, with one activity leading at a prearranged time into the next, the entire circle of activities being imposed from above through a system of explicit formal rulings and a body of officials. "The contents of the various enforced activities are brought together as parts of a single overall rational plan purportedly designed to fulfill the official aims of the institution."

The first weeks at The Pen, I was so focused on getting the library opened that I never fully realized how much Goffman's description portrayed the institutional life I entered each day. Prisoners had the same routine and a specific time and options for activities, all under the watchful jurisdiction of correctional officers. This included wakeup time, going to the dining hall, library, education building, assigned work areas, and visiting hours. In the recreational yard, activities included playing ballgames, sitting on the sidelines watching or "bullshitting" with the officers and other prisoners, sitting on the sidelines waiting for payment for past or a pending drug or other transaction. Other prisoners remained in their cells watching television, writing letters, attending various group meetings. At each location the correctional officers recorded and supervised all activities at designated times.

The Library Opens, March 1987

The colorful, positive, and welcoming atmosphere I visualized became a reality, largely due to the helpful responses from prisoners who gave the library some of their personal artwork, and the commitment of the prison library clerks to have the library opened. I gave priority to acquiring up-to-date legal and reference materials and used the general recreational and nonfiction collections books that I found in the boxes that were there prior to my arrival.

The first two weeks of opening, the library reached maximum capacity with visitors. Curiosity rather than information need was the lure. I hovered in the reading room area, behind the circulation, magazine, and reference desks, observing the clerks as well as answering questions from the visitors. Personal interactions and a suggestion box at the circulation desk provided me with more insights for information needs.

A daily pattern developed. The same individuals visited the library to read magazines, newspapers, or just to browse the shelves, very often not borrowing any materials. Others whom I described as "weather birds" came to the library on very hot or very cold days, air conditioning and heating being the lure, not information needs. These weather birds were often noisy and created distractions.

The jailhouse lawyers would strut in the library with folders and an air of authority to impress librarian and other prisoners. Many jailhouse lawyers had extensive knowledge of the law and legal materials, researching their cases, seeking appeals, or filing grievances against the administration, claiming violation of their constitutional rights. They constantly criticized the library for not meeting the requirements for "access to the courts." I would remind them that the library's legal collection was supplementary, since Maryland prison libraries were not "access to the courts." The jailhouse lawyers who assisted illiterate prisoners to research their cases earned lucrative payments for services rendered. Payments for any service rendered in the prison system took many forms: Predetermined number of sodas. Cigarettes. Commissary items. Artwork. Sex. Clothing. Having a family member on the outside collect money that is lodged in the prisoner's account. The debtor who does not pay becomes the victim of varying acts of violence and other punitive measures determined by the prison culture. Demonstrations of punitive retaliation for nonpayment earn the enforcer more respect and power.

The manipulators knew how to scan their environment and apply techniques they deemed appropriate for the expected outcomes. They used a variety of methods to get attention and achieve their goals. The good-looking, strong-muscled men strutted around complimenting female workers in a manner that often said, "I'm here for you, babe." Library clerks told me that this technique works among the female staff who have lots of competition "on the street," especially those who were not considered attractive. Humor and laughter would accompany the stories that some of the clerks shared about female officers who fall for the compliments. One of these stories included a female officer who sometimes just happened to be making security checks by the shower stall when certain prisoners were taking their showers.

These manipulators used various strategies. Initiating conversations about people they knew from the same neighborhood. Appearing to be on the side of the institution or a particular security staff. Sharing information about other prisoners. If they thought an officer's behavior showed preference towards a particular prisoner, they spread stories about inappropriate relationships. Those who appear as thoughtful and educated, not like "dem other hoods," positioned themselves and were often successful in getting more information during their interactions with staff. In some cases, they "tell staff in confidence" the happenings in the prison. Their goal is to be considered trustworthy since they were risking their personal safety by providing the information. These behaviors often earned the actors the best prison jobs, favoritism by staff, and respect or envy from other prisoners.

I wondered how I would survive in this fishbowl, where prisoners observed every movement, interaction, and responses, mentally recording everything for future opportunities. It did not take me long to become aware that they were watching my interactions with other prisoners and pushed me on some issues mostly to observe my reaction. I also heard that some prisoners made bets on expected outcomes when they baited staff.

Chapter 4
Librarian in Prison

The library profession emphasizes helping users to meet their information needs by creating a welcoming atmosphere so customers feel at ease in seeking, anticipating, and getting appropriate and satisfactory answers for their information queries. To ensure this, librarians conduct reference interviews, at times standing side by side or head to head with customers, as together they seek and examine the sources for the information. How did this play out in a prison environment rife with manipulation? I made sure I was never too physically close to a prisoner, and in a voice audible to others asked the seeker to repeat or write requests and return later for a response. Unlike libraries on the outside, the men lived on the same compound, a few steps from the library. They knew their court dates ahead of time, and I constantly reminded them that individuals with the earliest court dates would get priority.

In addition to the legal and leisure reading information needs, prisoners began asking for readers' advisory suggestions, which provided me with insights for collection development. During incarceration, many prisoners lose contact with friends and family members so family connections became important. There were conversations about their children, grandmothers, sisters, and mothers in that order. Some of them told me that their mothers had not been positive influence in their life, but their grandmothers had a special place. Others talked about protecting their sisters from "craziness on the street," and those with children said they did not want their children to repeat their mistakes. The library received many requests that sought help for family members on the outside. When I suggested that they encourage these family to visit their nearest local public libraries, where they would get more detailed information, their response was: " They don't use or go to the public library."

Some questions from the prisoners were: "My wife has some woman problem and needs surgery. She has no money, and she moved to D.C. Do you know of any free place there that she can go for the surgery?"

I researched and gave him a list for reduced or free medical care providers in the Baltimore Washington area.

"I have a daughter and I never deal much with her on the street. Now she is a teenager and I think she getting into sex, so I would like to give her some information."

I put aside thoughts that this may be a question to make me feel uncomfortable, walked with the seeker to the reference desk while conducting the reference interview to ensure the information provided was relevant to his requests. The library had insufficient information on this topic so I used Maryland Interlibrary Loan System, through the Enoch Pratt Free Library. The materials arrived a few weeks later and the requestor thanked me.

"My son is graduating from high school soon and I would like to know if you can help me find information about jobs and college funds, as I don't want him to come in here like me." After receiving many similar questions, the *Occupational Outlook Handbook* became a part of the library's reference collection. Some prisoners also used this book for their own education in preparation for their return to society.

"I really want information about the location of the moon around midnight on this date because the officer could not have been able to identify me based on the location of the moon."

This request took me a long time to find. I went to the public library and used their reference materials to photocopy some information. I also pointed out some headings he could research from the encyclopedias on the prison library reference shelf.

Some mothers of the children of incarcerated men had either moved out of state or did not want the children to visit the men in prison. These fathers wanted information on family law to determine how they could still get visitation rights. The constant disappearance and requests for books on starting your own business, calligraphy, painting, art, English grammar, sign language, self-esteem and self-exploration, GED, black history, and true crime became my informal surveys for the popular nonfiction categories. Puzzled by the high interest in books on sign language since I had no deaf patrons, I soon learned that it was a method of communication that corrections officers were unlikely to comprehend. For recreational reading, the younger prisoners wanted "street lit" like Donald Goines. Older prisoners were more interested in the nonfiction subjects, and titles on *The New York Times* bestseller list.

I asked one of the clerks, "Why is there so much interest in the true crime books?'

"Many of the books have details about court cases and defense. We like to read them to see if we can get some tips to use in the court for our own cases and our appeals," he replied.

The prison library served many purposes. It was a safe and quiet place for the prisoners who wanted alone time away from the bustle and noise of the cellblock or the recreation yard. It was a haven for the prisoner who was not a tough person and who wanted to avoid physical altercations with the bullies or the sex predators. It provided the men with opportunities to read about topics in which they were interested but had no previous access.

"On the street we never go to any library. We too busy doing other things, selling drugs, making money, entertaining the girls," they told me.

Most importantly, the library was the resource center for prisoners who did their own legal research either solo, or with help from cohorts or jailhouse lawyers. It was also a lucrative haven for the jailhouse lawyers, and the "businessman," as one prisoner described himself. While sometimes I found the demanding, arrogant, and sexist attitudes of some jailhouse lawyers annoying, the extent of their legal expertise was impressive. I had proof of this when I organized a program inviting law school students from a local university to engage in a debate with some prisoners. At the end of the program a few of the college students expressed surprise at the intelligence and depth of the legal knowledge of the prisoners. One young woman came to me, curious about the nature of the crimes, asking me when two of the participants would leave prison. I responded that majority of these men were lifers, some of whom may have executed dumb and inexcusable acts, but that did not necessarily reflect their intellectual capacity. I also used the opportunity to say that the root causes of many of their incarceration was due to economic inequities, lack of much support from a public defender, and racial injustices that perpetuated the poor black neighborhoods from which they came.

The daily ritual in the library was basically the same. Some users headed for the magazine and reference sections, presented their ID to the library clerk, requested a particular item from behind the desk, getting back the ID when they return the borrowed item. Others either sat by themselves or join a group. Yet others removed chairs from the tables and sat at the same nonfiction or fiction section every time. Mornings, the library was filled with users reading, seeking information, or just passing time. Some of them gave advice to others on what to read, others joked around, or to quote them, "just hanging out in the library." Afternoons, fewer patrons visited. They said they did not want to miss "the soaps" on television. A lively discussions on the previous day's TV viewing would often take place in the library. During football season, on Monday evenings, the library was quiet, almost empty. The pattern for visitors was so regular that absenteeism over a period generally meant illness, job acquisition somewhere in the institution, trying to avoid other prisoners, placement on protective custody, segregation, transfer to another prison or, the least likely, release from prison.

If someone was considered a snitch, his life may be in danger. Safety options were protective custody, segregation, transfer to another institution in Maryland, or to an out-of-state prison. Prisoners who were owed, asserted authority, power, and demand for respect by ensuring they received payment by any means necessary. This sometimes resulted in serious harm and violence to the debtors. The latter sometimes went on protective custody either in the prison or by being transferred to another institution. The most desirable and sought-after departure for prisoners, however, was transfer from The Pen to lesser-security institutions, a signal they were preparing for a return to society. Although rare, a prisoner may leave the institution on early release due to successful appeals. Such was the case of Kirk Bloodsworth, [7] who was sentenced to death but later exonerated after DNA proved his innocence. While prisoners may be aware of their eligibility to leave The Pen, they never know the exact date or time of departure. This was due to public safety's precaution to prevent jealousy and fights among the remaining prisoners, violent retaliation for unpaid debts, and/or to prevent prisoners from alerting family or friends on the outside to minimize escape attempts.

---

[7] Junkin, Tim. *Bloodsworth: The True Story of the First Death Row Prisoners Exonerated by DNA*. Chapel Hill: Algonquin Books of Chapel Hill, 2004.

The library received many letters from segregation units. Sometimes the prisoners were on "lock up" due to minor infractions and they often disputed the charges, accusing correctional staff of unfair practices. Requests from this group included information on institutional rules, forms to file grievances against the administration, and to appeal their segregation status. Those on segregation for long periods requested recreational reading materials, magazines, and newspapers. Prisoners who were illiterate sometimes sought and got help from the more knowledgeable among them, often at a price. If, however, the lock-up prisoner was a friend of or belonged to one of the prison groups, gang or organizations, his cohorts may do the research for free, with the expectation of future reciprocity. Detailed legal information requests often came from those on long-term segregation, death row, or those confined for life.

The prison system does not allow prisoners to have cash. Money is contraband. How then do prisoners pay for services rendered? Some of the non-monetary transaction amused and amazed me.

"That cost ten packs, man." In the 1980s, when smoking was allowed in the prison, cigarettes were among the most expensive and popular items of trade. One cigarette or a pack of cigarettes had a predetermined monetary value. When correction authorities banned smoking, cigarette price escalated. Instead of a pack, a single cigarette could cost one dollar. The ban on smoking did not deter the underground cigarette trade. Ever resourceful, those working outside the fence picked up cigarette butts (roadkill) from the street and sold them. They also got cigarettes and other items from the "mule," staff members who violated prison rule by doing favors for prisoners. Payment may be in the form of sex, predetermined illegal deals, clothes, shoes, commissary items, materials stolen from the work area, weapons, or items to make weapons, food from the kitchen, or prisoners' artwork.

Objects smuggled into the prison either by prisoners' family members or the "mules" were all articles of trade. There was one consistent rule among the prisoners.

"You must pay your debt, or you pay the price."

If punishment was not inflicted on the debtors, it meant the lender was weak, would lose credibility, and faced the possibility of eventually becoming a victim himself.

I was intrigued by the stories of prisoners stealing from their work locations and taking it to their cells.

"With all this security and so many officers all around the compound and in the cells, how can they steal things?" I asked.

"Easy, miss," one clerk replied. "You see how some of them guys wear coats and jackets, bigger than they real size? The jackets have plenty pockets, plus they cut out portions of the inside lining so they can stash things."

I later found out that these coats were also the hiding place for library books. When some library clerks alerted me to the prisoners who were stashing books in their clothing, or other safety issues, I knew that I had earned their trust. If anyone knew they told me, their life would be in danger.

"That guy keep walking out with books in his coat."

"Careful of that guy, Ms. S., 'cause him in here for sex offense."

"Ms. Shirley, you may want to take some vacation if you have some." A sign of impending unrest in the prison.

They told me that if I noticed that an unusual number of prisoners were opting not to go to work, the library, or to the dining room at mealtime, it was an indication that trouble was brewing as the individuals staying in their cells did not want to get involved in whatever was to take place.

One Year Later, 1988

The day I arrived at work and a clerk congratulated me for completing one year at The Pen, I laughed and said, "Wow, time flies and the amazing thing is that you are all still alive."

Another said, "When we go to our cellblock, Miss Shirley, the guys talk about how honest and helpful you are, and how you treat us with respect. So Ms. S., the library is safe."

I received the same sentiments on many occasions from other library users. Although loyalty and respect were generally more overtly among themselves, **prisoners** exercised their own codes of respect and protection on staff whom they liked. They told me that they discussed and determined which staff members earned their respect, and they put an invisible protective shield around them. Anyone who violated these protection codes would eventually be punished by their peers.

Did their comments make me relax? Not really. It made me more alert and wary of manipulation since compliments were survival and power tools that many used to gain acceptance and favors, especially from female staff. Orientation procedures and annual retraining sessions outlined various manipulative techniques and punitive consequences for violations on all sides. However, in an environment where staff and prisoners occupy the same space for at least eight hours each day, prisoners gain power by observing, listening, and asking seemingly innocent questions, banking for future exploitation, the strengths, weaknesses, and vulnerabilities that they observe among staff.

Prison Library Programs

To create awareness of community and national issues that the prisoners said they previously had no interest, and to engage in more institutional collaborations, I initiated a variety of programs. To get support and some collaboration among the education instructors, I said to them, "For Black History Month, it would create more educational awareness if some of your students write essays about Martin Luther King. I will display these essays in the library. This should be a great self-esteem booster for the men. I am also hoping to organize an afternoon event where some of them read their essays at a gathering."

The pride on the face of the men who had their essays on display in the library was priceless. It was the first time they had ever received positive recognition. One of the men, Gary, who was illiterate when he entered prison, became a library fan after he got the opportunity to display and read the essay that he wrote.

HAPPY BIRTHDAY MARTIN LUTHER KING, by Gary

I been dying for this day to come in my life when I could write or say something good about a great man such as yourself.

Sorry to say that at the time you were fighting for a better education for the illiterate, I was out the back door of the school thinking it was hip. I thought sure that nothing would turn this world around. Yes, you were fighting against the discrimination. I was in the alley drinking wine with my buddy singing, "Say it loud, I'm black and I'm proud." But not as proud as you. It really takes a proud man to stand in the light and walk as our Lord did.

Keeping your dream alive—I would like to say we have people all around the world with open hearts helping illiterates such as I to read and write. Yes, you have opened many doors to people like me.

Yes, and did you know that people in the Maryland Penitentiary prisons are walking for sickle cell anemia, keeping your dream alive? I know that if you were here, this would put a big smile on your face. Keeping your dream alive means lots of doors open for the homeless, and today people are really opening doors for them. This really makes my heart glad.

If you were here, I would really like to know what you are feeling inside. We love you and are keeping your dream alive.

Gary.

Programs with outside guests require lots of security protocols and approval. I sought and got permission to invite guest speakers from legal firms, newspapers, actors, and musicians. One of the guest speakers, a well-known Baltimore lawyer, began to use profanities during his presentation. Several prisoners expressed indignation because they said he only resorted to that kind of language, thinking he had to go down to their level. They said they were even more offended because the lawyer was disrespecting the teaching and library staff by using such profanities.

Stevie Wonder, the Motown singing entertainer, was one of outstanding national guests the prison administration invited to The Pen. The prisoners were thrilled to be part of this historic memorable event that took place in the prison gym.

My Musings

Watch Your Language

It is lunchtime. Classes are over. The library is closed. This period without direct contact with prisoners gives me the opportunity to sit at my desk and work on files, make phone calls, and do clerical tasks. The men are in the library area waiting for permission to leave the building. They are exchanging jokes, news, gossips, talking about events, personalities, and women. I often overhear some of what they are talking about and this gives me great insight into happenings in prison. Today their loud interchange is laced with profanities. I get up, quietly open my office door, stand behind the circulation desk, look towards the area where they are standing and talking.

"Gentlemen," I say in a calm but firm voice, loud enough for all to hear, "while you may declare that it is your constitutional rights to use profanities and curse words, I also have a constitutional right not to have to listen to you shouting profanities so loudly in the library space. I would really appreciate if you refrain in my presence."

"Sorry," someone replies.

After that I never hear them use profanities around me. Several weeks later, as I return from lunch, several prisoners in the lobby area are talking and joking, and using profanities with one another, and with the female officer on duty. As I walk by, one of them says, "Man, don't you see the lady passing? Watch your language."

The Eyes

The library period and instructional hours are over. Library users and classroom students congregate inside at the entrance of the library, across from my office. They are waiting for the officer's permission to exit the building for lunch. Most days I remain at my desk until they leave. Today I am aware of a pair of eyes boring into me. Looking out, I see a guy standing by the glass window with an intense fixed gaze. My glass cage protects me. The correctional officer is at the entrance so any movement on his part to enter my cage would be detrimental to his future. I'm not scared. He knows and I know.

I look up and the pair of eyes impales me with their impassive intensity. Feigning unconcern, I lower my head and continue to work. I am sitting behind my desk in an office surrounded by glass built for transparency to ensure security. Everyone can see everything. I rise from my desk, pull open a file drawer, and extract a file, knowing that the eyes are following my every movement. Now, however, there is not only one pair of eyes, but what seems to me like dozens. Herd-like, they stand silently staring.

God, I think to myself, *Now I know how the fish in an aquarium feels. Next time I visit an aquarium I definitely will show more respect for their feelings and need for privacy.*

I return to the desk and sit down, aware that the eyes are following me, how many pairs now, I do not know. A slight tilt of my head upward shows that at least six pairs of those eyes are pressed against the glass looking in my cage, not with childlike curiosity but with the appraising look of man to woman. Those eyes belong to men, grown men who dare not enter my cage because they themselves are caged. My glass cage is pleasant with a nice desk, plants, shelves with books, low enough that I can always see and be aware of what is going on around me. I can leave whenever I wish. They, on the other hand, cannot get out from behind the walls or their metal cages that will be their only home for several years or for the duration of their life. These visible cages helped construct the cages of their own minds, an impediment that may last a lifetime. I continue my scrutiny of the files, then begin to type.

My intruding thoughts ask, *Am I being undressed to keep some sexual fantasy alive? Am I a reminder of a past existence outside those walls that now keep them locked in? What do I represent, a sister, a mother, a lover, a friend, someone to touch, to love to swear at, to hurt or whom they have hurt? What role do I play behind those staring eyes?*

My fingers never waver as I type. My thoughts, however, travel much faster as I ponder the questions. I know that the eyes never wavered either, because each time I look up, they are still staring.

"FEED UP," comes the welcome shout from the officer on duty.

With those words, the herd, like a well-rehearsed performance, surges forward in unison to the next phase of their daily ritual. Lunch in the prison dining room. The door slams behind the last person as he exits.

Phew! I'm alone in the library. Now I can scratch that itch and move around freely.

Chapter 5

The Prisoners

Sam

He is tall, scraggly looking, with eyes, nose, and mouth barely seen through the mountain of hair on his face and head. His faraway look gives the impression he is out of tune with his surroundings. Whenever I speak to Sam, he takes a long time responding, as if deciding whether or not to answer. I never knew whether he was pondering my question, or burying his resentment of a situation where I, a female, is in the superior role. As an action-oriented person with little tolerance for male chauvinism, I find it difficult to stand around waiting for his leisurely response. However, in this setting of extreme sensitivity and need for respect, his feelings would be hurt if I just walk away or display impatience. I certainly hope my personality does not get warped by this unnatural world to which I have voluntarily entered in exchange for a biweekly envelope that assures a roof over my head.

"You don't realize that most of us guys have never worked before," he says as he looks at me, expecting some response. "Before you, I never cared about my job. You get a lot out of most of us guys."

I listen without responding but later, in my usual self-analytical mode, I ask myself,   "Am I wrong in not lavishing them with the praise that they appear to need so much?"

By normal standards, many of them are not great workers but they expect to receive praise for everything they do. They also want me to reward them for just showing up for work in the library. Most of them fight attempts to follow rules and procedures, conforming only to the extent their actions will not negatively hamper their criminal records. Am I being unfair? Their behaviors were not unlike some people on the outside, and as he said, they had never done any traditional work before entering prison. On the streets, in their hustle for survival and to gain supremacy, they made up their own rules and codes of discipline. I recall a previous conversation with Sam.

"It started with petty thievery when we steal because we were hungry. Then it became easy and we took more things. Then we were daring one another as to who could take the most under the most challenging situation. Later it give us a certain sense of power. I could walk into a store and come out with a thousand-dollar coat in a matter of minutes. It did not make sense to work like a slave at some job at McD's for about $4 an hour. Dressed in my expensive coat, clothes and with all my rings and chains, Miss S.," he paused, opened his eyes wide, emphasizing the next words to show the power those clothes gave him. "I could have any girl or woman I want." He sat quietly for a moment, as if he had nodded off. Then he roused himself and continued. "Yes, the women were there just ready for me and the other guys. The more expensive you look, the more choices you have. I was young. That was the life. I had no incentive to work. The future was so far away. In the sixties, I joined the Civil Rights Movement, and did everything the young people did in those days. I tried every form of drugs." His tone became reflective, his eyes looked beyond the room as he continued.

"I think that a lot of the things I can't remember now is the result of my experiments with all those drugs." He said this in a tone as if he had expected me to contradict him. "It must have affected my brain, Miss S."

I responded that many of us forget things as we age. "For example," I said, "I have to write down almost everything, since I am apt to forget, and I never took any form of drugs except what the doctor ordered."

He gets up abruptly from the chair, walks out the office to his work desk in the other section of the library. I sit in quiet reflection, knowing that in a few minutes another prisoner will be seeking my attention to begin another conversation. I often feel like I am a parent to these prisoners whose childlike behaviors demand so much attention. They make up excuses to come into my office, showing off to others that they have my attention. They are hurt if I treat or dismiss them lightly and they are quick to shift the blame if they think their action may result in negative consequences. They expect to get praises for the simplest act.

Hmm, I think. *I feel I'm turning into a counselor and psychologist.* This thought takes me to another conversation with Sam.

"I am 42 years old, Ms. S., and I have been in and out jail for over 25 years. I have a daughter who is 22 years old. I remember the nice times we had when she was a baby. I really love her. What can I say to her now?" He gave the desk a light pound with his clenched fist. "I am a hardened criminal. How can I tell her not to do something? I am no example!"

"Maybe you could use yourself as an example of what not to be," I had replied.

Card from Sam

Ms Shirley:

"It is now only residually 1987, and like images in
an heirloom photographs of childhood's anticipation,

the holiday season develops in my mind's eye: ghost of memory but good ones.

These figments I wish for and share with you ......So with you and your family, may the principles of Kwanzaa supercede those of Murphey's Law. Please have a festive Harvest Feast."

Conversations with Sam brought awareness of some of the issues I encountered with other prisoners. Majority of these grown men had never done traditional work. Prior to incarceration they were their own bosses for the most part.

"On the street selling dope, I was a businessman who knew my market. If I'm not out on the street at a certain time, the competitor will come and take away my business," one of them said to me.

It was often the retaliatory responses to someone treading on their territory that landed many of these men in the prison system. Some of them shared stories about their personal life. They did not grow up with their mothers. They never had to deal with women as authority figures. Most of the women in their daily life were those in a subordinate role. These women tried to please the men as they are rewarded with money, and expensive purchases. Their female partners were in prison because they broke the law to please them.

El, a prisoner who converted to Islam after his incarceration, told me that he had difficulty dealing with me since he had never encountered an intelligent black woman before. I never regarded his statement as offensive because he said this without acrimony or malice. It was his reality. El and I developed mutual respect for each other. He would ask me questions on a variety of topics like Jamaican history, United States culture, racism, class, and poverty. I answered the questions as best I could, knowing they were sincere. I used these interactions to introduce relevant reading materials in the library. He and other prisoners told me that this was the first time in their life someone was taking time to converse with them on these issues. At times they made statements that I never quite knew whether I should laugh or lecture. El, for example, said that with the American genocide of the black race, it was valid to have as many children as possible to ensure black survival.

Before entering prison, my cultural indoctrination was that women gossiped. In prison, I was surrounded by majority male staff and prisoners who entertained me not only with all the gossip, but they also shared prison information that I found useful. Their varied work assignments provided the incarcerated men with lots of access to conversations on the telephone, intercom, among staff, and among their peers. I heard about love affairs of some officers, family situations, female staff and questionable relationship with prisoners, homosexual tendencies, and unreasonable and unfair behaviors towards the prisoners. I found the gossip and speculations amusing because the men included their own salacious and humorous interpretations on every situation.

Tee

I look up. His eyes lock into mine. I stand and walk to the front of the room, aware that his eyes are following me. When I return he is still staring with a silent intensity that makes me uncomfortable. He is always polite, never engaging in frivolous remarks nor did he walk, play or interact in groups or cliques like his fellow prisoners. He is always by himself, reading most of the time. I did not reply to his initial application for a position as a library clerk because of my feelings of discomfort regarding his intense staring. One year goes by. He tells me he is still waiting for a job in the library. I decide to be frank.

"I have not considered your application because you make me uncomfortable. Every move I make you follow me with your eyes, just staring. I conclude you have a problem, and it would be best if I did not hire you."

He looks at me, eyes widening in surprise. "I had no idea I was doing that, miss. I guess it's because I have been confined in this place for so long. You are a beautiful woman. It's not often we see someone like you around and I guess I was admiring you. I never meant for you to feel uncomfortable. If you only give me a chance, now that I am aware, I will try not to do it again."

I hire him. He is a very efficient worker, first to arrive at work and last to leave. He has minimal interactions with other library clerks, or to my knowledge, with the general population. In the prison environment, arriving early and leaving last at a work location gives prisoners opportunities to store, hide, or retrieve contraband. It could also be a manipulative ploy to impress a staff member for future gains. Aware of this, I try to keep a close watch on the library clerks, fully aware that they could outsmart me any time. To my knowledge none of them violated rules.

Tee is no longer staring. He seeks my attention by asking nonessential job-related questions that I know he is smart enough to resolve on his own. Aware that this may be his way to engage my attention, I give terse responses. His tactics change. He is now bringing magazine articles, saying he figured I could use them for future projects. He brings me poems that he wrote, asking my opinion. Sometimes I read them, other times I say that I am busy and would get to them later. Accustomed to the clerks greeting me as they enter the library, I sometimes respond before they finish the greeting. For example, "Good morning...." "How are you today, John?" I often ask before John completes his greeting.

The morning Tee greeted me with, "Hello, beautiful."

I had already responded with, "Good morning, Tee," before I realized his form of greeting.

I did not want to bring further attention so did not react to indicate my annoyance. I resolved to be more alert the next time. I avoided him most of that day. One morning he asked to speak to me. I said okay. He came into my office, sat in the chair to the right of my desk, in clear view of all prisoners who were looking through the glass.

"I know you said I used to stare, and I explained that most of us in here have never learned how to behave morally. I have been incarcerated for 15 years and I had no one to teach me anything good. My mother was a whore and therefore was no example." He shifted in the chair adopting a very relaxed pose, as he continued. "I notice when I talk to you, you recoil and pull away. Yet when you talk to the other guys you are always laughing and act comfortable with them. I would like you to treat me the same way. We may be criminals, but we are also human beings."

"First, " I replied, "the others have earned my being relaxed with them. I have worked with them for over a year and I know what to expect from each person. I can make any joke with them and they have never been vulgar, made any sexual references in my presence, or go into any of those sexual innuendos that are so typical, common, and tiresome in this environment. Nor do they make me feel uncomfortable. I came here to do a job. Professionalism is important to me. That takes precedence. You mentioned 'invisible barriers' in one of your poems. To me they are not invisible. They are real and upfront. The men in here are prisoners. There are codes of rules and conduct governing staff and prisoners' behavior. I have no intention of violating them. I expect the prisoners with whom I come in contact to behave the same way. That is the rule of the game, and that is how I plan to operate."

Then the following words tumbled out my mouth.

"The other day you greeted me with 'Hello, beautiful.' My name is Miss Shirley. That is how I expect to be addressed. I don't care what you did to get in here, I don't care about your background, and I don't care what your sexual fantasies are. My name is Miss Shirley, and that is how I expect you and the other prisoners to address me."

He left the office shaking his head, smiling, giving the impression that we had just shared something in common.

Tee continues to bring in poems and articles, and is more than willing to do any task I require. I know he would do an excellent job, but didn't make as many requests of him as I did the others. I do not dislike Tee. I respect his professionalism. My reaction is due to my gut feeling of discomfort, and the likelihood of his misinterpreting any relaxed behavior on my part. The clerks noticed some of his behavior pattern and one of them said to me, "Ms. S., I have no reason to be saying this, but I don't feel comfortable with Tee around. He had the best job in the institution where he could get anything and no one would touch him. I am puzzled why he gave up all this to come and work in the library. I don't trust him, Ms. S. I am leaving this institution in a week or so, I would feel more comfortable if you rehired RC, who you just fired. RC's presence would prevent him from trying anything."

The fact that this prisoner was leaving the institution and had nothing to gain increased my caution. I made sure I was never in a place alone with Tee, moving to areas within reach of other prisoners. I also never accepted his constant offers of candies or oranges. One day he came into my office asking if he could speak. I said yes.

"As I explained to you the other day, Miss Shirley, many of us in here are without morals because we never learned any, but some of us are trying. It is difficult, though, because of some of the women workers we encounter in this place. For example, many of these women do not get a lot of attention on the street and in here the men tell them a lot of things and they accept it or contribute to it. For example, Ms. Shirley, I hope I don't offend you by what I am going to say, but if you are offended you can stop me. Last night I was in the shower masturbating and a female officer came and just stood right beside me. She said that when I was uptown, I must have made some female happy. When I asked her what she meant, she referred to my size, and to tell you the truth, Ms. Shirley," he said with a smile that gave the impression he was telling a secret, "I'm proud of my size, if I may say so myself. Then she was telling me that if I want her she was up on the 4th tier."

"I imagine you are intelligent enough to distinguish between different types of persons," I said, as he rose and left my office with a smile and a strut.

Tee had a personal subscription to a newspaper approved by the prison. Some days he left his newspaper in my office when he went to lunch because he did not wish other prisoners to steal it. The name "TEE" was always written on the upper-right corner. The day after his conversation about size, as he was leaving for lunch, he stretched the paper towards me, saying there was an interesting article I may like. In the spot where he normally put his name were the words "BIG TEE."

The morning Tee did not report for work the clerks told me he was on lockup. One night he was so drunk and staggering that an officer had to lead him to his cell. They said it was a relief that he was out of the way because he was too arrogant, behaving as if he thought he was better than them instead of being a prisoner just like them. The prison grapevine said that Tee managed to collect his money for the packets of marijuana he had distributed prior to lockup.

After his ten-day stint on lockup, he returned to the library. This time he started wearing sweatpants that displayed his phallic projection. Sometimes when I was seated at my desk, he would enter my office to ask a question, braced his hip forward, with arms folded, as if concentrating on his question or my answer. This seemingly innocent posture, feet apart, placed anything below his waist in direct line with my eyes. How did I cope with this? A brusque reply. Stand up, so we were eye to eye instead of eye to crutch, and I would move towards the door as I responded to his question. I was aware that if I said anything he may interpret it that I was noticing him. If I said nothing, he may consider it as silent acquiescence. He was never rude, came to work on time, I did not have to worry about losing any material under his watch and he was diligent. He was also a good and dependable worker. I instinctively knew that in the library, the reference collection would remain intact under his watch. My discomfort was his supposedly harmless attempt at getting closer to me in what I considered a more personal way.

TEE'S Birthday card:

Birthday wishes for you Ms. Glennor Shirley
Into a world full of darkness
You brought us the light.
A poetic intelligence
That brightened our sight.
With unselfish diplomacy
You gave to us all;
The knowledge of your profession
To help us stand tall.
Heaven sent to us a blessing
The day of your birth
Wearing the crown of dignity

The Spitter

He was very short and small bodied. He walked around the prison yard with glazed eyes, matted hair, dirty clothes, and an odor emanating from him that would make you hold your nose and walk rapidly in the opposite direction. He walked everywhere holding a cup filled with spittle. Prisoners and officers said this was his way of protecting himself against sexual assault.

The Career Criminal (CC)

CC is among the older prisoners, short in stature with long matted hair. He never creates problems in the library. He tells me that he is amused by the antics of the "young guys" and often gives me hints about the behaviors and expectations from certain prisoners. I feel comfortable enough with him to pose the question that supervisors instructed us never to ask prisoners.

"What are you in here for?"

He straightens his shoulders, tosses his head from which matted and twisted hair hang below his shoulder.

"I'm what they call a career criminal, " he replies with an expression that shows pride in this occupation.

I look at him as he continues.

"There's not a safe that I couldn't open. No, there are only two types that gave me some problems, but if I had more time, I would have been able to master them as well. I lived well." His eyes take on a far-away look. "I had two apartments and a fancy sportscar. I could buy anything I want. Yes, the life was good."

It is clear from the dreamy look in his eyes that he is now out of his present confines and into the world of the career that landed him in

The Pen. He remains silent. Suddenly he returns to his present environment and looks at me, expecting some reaction.

"Why?" I ask.

"I was a bad guy from youth. My parents gave up on me. I never listened to them and I just hung around the guys who always get into trouble. I went to prison several times."

"Wasn't the experience bad enough for you not to want to return?"

The dreamy look returns. "After a while the police would pick up my friends and take them to jail. There was no one to hang around with. You visit them—yes, but still, you're lonely without them, so you do something that the police would pick you up and jail you too. In jail we were all together. You know after all, the jail become like a second home. If you get out, you don't have any skill. You like the luxurious life so you just go back to the life you were familiar with. I'm an old man now. I'll soon be sixty-one years old. I have no one to blame for what I became. My parents were good people. I just did not want their style of life."

I look at him. "Does any family member visit you?"

He shakes his head, his matted locks scattering in all directions. "No, and I prefer it that way. I'm an embarrassment to them. I chose my way of life and that's just the way it is." His tone is matter-of-fact. No bitterness, just reflective. He continues. "You will find there's a difference between me and these young guys in here. They be bitter about so many things, they all trying to be so macho, but at heart they just like anybody else. They want to talk to you. They want a little mothering, and just a little attention. They don't want the others to see them as weak, so they put on this big macho stuff."

His eyes take on that dreamy look again and he is silent. Suddenly he says in a businesslike tone, "Well, I must leave you to get on with your work. Tomorrow I'll take the Pledge and shine the desk for you."

64

He shakes his locks, makes a sharp right turn through the door, gently closes the outer gate, and moves towards his companions. A few minutes later, I look out and see his head is buried in his usual spot above the low bookshelf, turning the pages of a book with his favorite subject. Esoteric literature.

A few weeks after our conversation, the media reported some incident in the Frederick Mall.

"Frederick Mall?" he says. "Oh, yes, I know where that is. As a matter of fact, I burgled that mall once."

"Were you caught?" I ask.

"No."

"Weren't you ever scared when you did those burglaries?"

"The first time I was scared like hell, because I had this big hammer hammering, and it sounded to me like the whole world could hear. I stopped several times but the dude who was with us just told me to keep on going. You develop a system. After a time we realized that the police patrols had about a fifty-mile radius to cover. They estimate that all burglaries take place between 3-5 A.M. We watch them and then aim for the place they patrol first. It means that unless someone call them for something, they will not be patrolling the area for another two or more hours. We have Walkie-Talkie and we post our men all over. They warn us if they see or hear anything suspicious. So sometimes we make a lot of noise when trying to open safes, or knocking down a door. Many malls don't have houses nearby so no one hear these noise and by the time the police come back we already on our way. It was a real challenge to do these things. The hint of danger is from being caught—loading the van with goods. We made thousands in a night. I operated in Delaware, Pennsylvania, and Maryland. I think I did something in Virginia and D.C. too. Oh, the life was real challenging," he says as he twirls his dreadlocks.

"What happened when you were caught, did they take all the stuff from you?"

"Oh, yes, I had two homes and cars, there was no record of my working. They sold some of the things and paid some of the people I stole from."

A few days later, he gives me a tiny card with the words: "*Your Friendship is a blessing.*" One Friday afternoon, he walks into the library and laughingly says to me, "Let me look at you and set my heart right for the weekend."

The following Monday, when I arrive at work, the clerks inform me that he died from a heart attack over the weekend. He was 61 years old. His alienation from the family meant that the corrections department would bury him in the prison cemetery. A fellow prisoner said he deserved better than that. This prisoner asked his family to take charge of the body and bury him.

"This way," the prisoner said, "there is some dignity instead of him being in an unknown grave." Several other prisoners donated money towards his burial. The first few months after his death, I missed seeing those dreadlocks among the "esoteric" section, his words of wisdom, and protective warnings. I placed the beautifully handmade card he gave me, on my desk. The words inside the card said:

I know not what the future holds
But I am glad
that you have
Enriched my Past.
"Thank You"
For simply being "you'…
Best Wishes Always

Cal

What can I say about Cal, the tall, slender prisoner with dreadlocks below his shoulder, a style that had not yet gained popularity? Praise. Accolades. Thanks. He was among my first library workers at The Pen. He never talked much but I sensed he was observing my every movement, decisions, and actions. He had great wit and intelligence and, in his quiet way, commanded a lot of respect among other prisoners. It was Cal who told me that he was not an inmate as that name indicates passivity. He preferred to be called "Prisoner," a name I try to use after this statement. Cal was one of the first two prisoners to graduate with a degree from Frostburg University in 1992.

To avoid the likelihood of rule violations and engagement in personal relationships, the prison administration warn staff not to rely or depend too much on any prisoner. In the prison atmosphere, however, watching your back and dealing with manipulators and snitchers, it is inevitable that staff at almost every level rely on and place some trust in a few prisoners. Cal and I developed mutual respect. I depended on him for a lot of prison wisdom and I knew he was watching my back. He educated me about the Black Panthers and black history, since as a new American immigrant I was not very familiar with African-American history and culture.

When Cal knew that he would be transferring to another institution, he warned me to be careful with whom I place any trust, and what I should do in the case of problems. After his departure, I missed his quirky, quiet humor, our discussion on politics, his always looking out for me, and his trustworthiness. I received several letters from him.

Letters from Cal: 2/4/88

Ms Shirley

Hi, I am doing fine and the family is slowly pulling itself together after mom's passing. Thanks for the cards. The warm thoughts expressed therein will always be cherished. Again, thanx!!

I got a letter from Rxx ystdy. He informed me that Ms J. has quit and that you may be leaving within 3-4 months. I'm glad that Ms. Jackson quit. I'd always felt that she was not strong enough to cope with the environment there. And it is good that she left before it put an indelible scar on her humanitarianism- if she had any and if it has not already happened.

Who do you have besides Lee who is as weak as fruitloops—to work with? Is Zee still on the magazine desk, or has he flown the coop also? I've always been concerned with women working in maximum security "male" prisons—especially those good hearted one like you (and sister ME)—who cannot fight at all! Smile

FYI. Red tried to stay until you left.

And where are you going? Home to Jamaica, I hope. Now that Seaga and the JLP have been defeated, perhaps Michael Manley and the people's National Party can continue with their program. What do you, by the way, think of Manley?

One last thing (Dirty Rb) said to tell you that Ms. Sing said she called you about him and you told her that Rob never worked for you- is there any truth to that?

STAY IN TOUCH

Your friend. Cal

Cal: 10/28/88
P.O. Box 2000
Well, HELLO, X-Boss LADY

Did I ever tell you that you were the first woman I have ever had as a boss? Well, you were—and I had intended to write you sooner and thank you for the rewarding experience, but my "Alzheimers" acted up. I planned to write later but my discipline broke down. So I am trying to write now but big brother bothers me.

One of the first thing I did after I arrived was to check-out the library. The Librarian, MS S. has a reputation similar to MS J. when she first arrived at the Pen. The library is a little hole-in-the-wall, although it does have a workable A/V section, reference & Legal section. The whole library will fit in the Pen Library 2-3 times. Also it is almost inaccessible to the general population. We can only go once a week by pass, and we must sign up in advance (when we go to breakfast at 5:00am). In other words, if we don't go to breakfast, we don't go to the library. How this could ever have been denoted the "best" library in the MD. DOC. Is beyond me. Even when the Pen Library was closed, we had better service than this.

Still I would have went to work there—as a matter of fact, I did apply for a temporary job, and gave Mrs. S. your letter of recommendation (with which she was greatly impressed)—but up here we cannot be enrolled in an educational/vocational program and work also.

And since I had enrolled in the High-Tech program, I couldn't work in the library. She did, however put my application on "hold" and said if I was still interested after I finish my shop program she would give me a job. As you know, I enjoy library service so I may consider it-if I am unfortunate as to be here for any significant amount of time.

The Parole Commission sent a psychologist up here to conduct an evaluation of me last month-prior to making a decision as to whether or not to give me an early parole re-hearing date. The evaluation went excellent and the psychologist said he "could see no reason why I should not be paroled." Neither can I.

Here we cannot have any pictures, posters or banners on our cell walls. We can have them on our lockers (18"x20"x4') so I have my JAMAICA poster/banner and my good-luck card on its door . A touch of class and a burst of sunshine! I received your criticism re. my sketches-what means your comment about my model's complexion? That seems out of character.

Have you decided how much more time you are going to serve?

Give Mrs. J., Mr. Murphey, and his staff & your staff my regards—especially.

Cal

After I left The Pen, Cal was among the many prisoners from whom I received letters at my new workplace.

Cal: 6/16/92

MCTC

Hi Friend

Damn, it was good to hear from you. I'd hear rumors about your whereabouts and the reason for leaving the Pen. Of course I kept an open mind and didn't believe any of it. I did, however, find the one about you and Brandy having words and a fight rather attractive. Now that you've enlightened me again, I do recall you saying something about quitting after a certain period of time. I hope your current employer appreciates you as much as your family here in DOC. I also hope you realize the number of prisoners you had a positive affect upon.

Many of them, John B., Howard, Mausa, Randy, Salim, McLean, and others, are always asking me if I heard from you, and how you and yours are doing—especially Randy and Mausa.

My family is doing okay, with the exception of my youngest son who is 16 and lives with his mother in North Carolina. It seems he is trying 'very hard" to follow in my footsteps—the ones I made when I was young and dumb. He has made me a grandfather and is living life in the fast lane, "so he thinks". He just finished doing 8 months in a juvenile prison, and I really think he will be in adult prison within the next 24 mts. He and I write and talk on the phone, but he is in that phase of saying what he thinks I want to hear so our communication is slow.

I finally got my B.S. from Frostburg State University! Hopefully, I will be released when I go up for Parole in '94. If not then soon thereafter. I cut my dreadlocks, got 'em in a box under my bed.

Revolutionary strength and Love
Cal

PS. You know whenever I think about you I smile and feel good! Thanx!!!

In case you lose track of me... (wife's address ....xxx)

A handmade card whose cover had a drawing of Bob Marley.

... Glennor, Your concern and support
Through the years will ever be appreciated.
Thank you
The Parole Board gave me an 18 month set-off
Hopefully, I'll be released in 9/95
Peace & Love,
Cal

January 24, 1999

In January 1999, Cal's companion and partner sent a letter to family and friends. In her letter she wished everyone Happy New Year, saying that her recap the year that was the "happiest year of my life."

She gave details of Cal's parole at the end of '97. "We have been a couple for the 14 preceding years, despite his moving from one end of the state to another in the Maryland prison system." She mentioned her daughter's delight at seeing her mom so happy, listed certain events that makes one realize the difficulty when prisoners transfer back to society.

Some events included two weeks after his parole, getting news that his brother who lived on the West Coast was dying from cancer, family members putting funds together to enable him to travel, and his fortune in getting permission from the Department of Corrections to travel out of state, where they were together for the funeral.

Shortly after they became first-time house owners, she was laid off from her job of seven years, but her new job was more lucrative.

Cal also united with a son for the first time, and connected with family members from the Carolinas to Delaware, videotaping some family history with elder family members.

Cal's handwritten postscript at the end of the letter said:

"Life is so much richer and fuller than the previous 26 years of captivity implied"—Cal.

Just Another Day

Don't Do That: The Instructor's Scream

A scream resounded from her two-hundred-plus frame. Swift as an arrow the prisoners catapulted from their desks in the classroom and sprinted towards the door with hands in the air. They spread eagled themselves against the wall, hands up, legs apart, heads turned towards the instructor, puzzled looks on their faces.

"A cockroach," she sputtered, pointing to the ground.

Breathing sighs of relief, the men returned to the room, this time with hands at their sides.

"Don't ever do that again, miss," one of them said to the instructor. "When you scream like that, the officers will run inside because they think we harming you."

The clerk who told me this story of his experiences in the correctional education classroom was still laughing when he recounted the incident.

Don't Do That: Brushing My Hair

"Don't do that. Don't do that."

I heard this loud whisper, with feigned desperation in the voice.

I looked up to see half a dozen pairs of eyes, wary, hungry, speculating, amused. Looking in my direction.

"What's the matter?" I asked, puzzled.

The simple, guileless reply came from one of the library clerks.

"Trev was getting excited, Ms. Shirley. Is such a long time since any of us see a woman comb her hair."

I had just returned from lunch, running a comb through my wind-blown shoulder-length hair. A few prisoners, including library workers, were inside the entrance area, waiting for the officer's permission to go upstairs to class or to enter the library. I had not considered my glass cage, nor realized the impact of simply brushing my hair in view of men who were confined for long periods. They never saw me comb my hair again.

Work Clothes. Titty Tat.

Overhearing the constant chatter and comments among the men about the clothing and dress habits of some of the female staff, I took great care in selecting my work clothes. I wore professional-looking outfits and each day, before leaving for work, I checked every button to ensure they were secure, tucked a safety pin in my skirt waist, in case a button should fall loose, double-checked my stockings more than once a day to assure there were no holes. I certainly did not want some very helpful prisoner enjoying my discomfort when he tells me that I had holes in my stockings. Nor did I want a name like the moniker they conferred on one of the female instructors, **"Titty Tat."** This instructor sometimes wore lowcut blouses that displayed the tattoo on the upper section of her breast. Behind her back and among themselves the prisoners referred to her as "Titty Tat."

From the Yard: Prisoners Fight

"10-10 in 4 yard by the school," the words came over the corrections officers' radio, indicating that some prisoners were fighting among themselves. The officer for the education building moved towards the door and looked out. Few minutes later, she opened the door and shouted, "All of them."

"What was that about?" I asked.

"Four men jumped Eric Sneed," she laughed, "but he defend hisself well."

Later I learned that Eric, the toucher, had exposed himself to one of the female hospital workers. The prisoners were angry about this disrespect to a staff member they liked, and they executed their own form of punishment on Eric.

Officers in the Staff Lunch Room

"Why didn't they kill his ass? Wouldn't be no need to take him to the hospital," one officer said.

They were talking about the prisoner who claimed that in the shower, he slipped on a bottle that lodged up his rectum. Lots of laughter followed this story, as each person concocted his or her own interpretation. For a few weeks, this incident was fodder and entertainment among prisoners and staff.

Count Time

Count time is one of the most important and perhaps the most stressful activity in the prison. It is the time when security staff count the number of prisoners in place to ensure there is no escape. Miscounts result in stress, especially if this occurs during a shift change when some officers are getting ready to leave. Stories the clerks tell me about count time problems include potential escapee creating huge humanlike dolls and propping up pillows in the bed under covers to give the appearance of being asleep when the officers check in. They said there was one successful short-term escape using this method. Majority of those trying to escapes even with careful planning were apprehended, especially those trying to escape over the fence. These incidences resulted in dress codes changes for prisoners. Each plain-colored shirt now had "DOC" boldly labelled on the back.

Officer Attacked

Seated at my desk one morning, I heard a chilling scream followed immediately by an eerie silence among the library clerks and users. As the screams continued, my head jerked up and I saw two prison library clerks standing by my door with gritted teeth as they muttered, "Stay inside."

I looked towards the officer for help, then realized she was the person who was screaming while a prisoner stood above her with stabbing motions. Remembering our training, I grabbed the phone to call for help. My hands were shaking. As I stood looking through the glass, motionless, I truly understood the meaning "paralyzed with fear." Did anyone answer the telephone? Did I dial the correct number? I can't recall. My hands were shaking as I looked helplessly on, scared, not knowing if this was a riot, if I would be next victim, or if library clerks standing by my door were among the rioters.

Suddenly I heard running footsteps and sounds other than the officer's screams. I looked out towards the entrance and saw corrections officers in the area where the officer was screaming. They had heard the screams and rushed downstairs. As they called for backup, like a well-rehearsed play, the previously immobile prisoners in the library rushed towards the door with a posture of helping the officer. I learned later that in the prison culture they would not place their life in danger by openly assisting an officer. However, once officers and reinforcements were on the spot, the appearance of helping the staff would likely place them in a favorable position among the officers, or when they appeared before the parole and probation board.

The report about the incident stated that the attacker wanted to visit the library but the officer on duty denied him access. They began exchanging profanities and he attacked her with a pen. Many prisoners said the officer was a foul-mouthed person who often spoke very disrespectfully to them, so she had it coming to her. They placed the attacker on segregation for a few months. The officer's injury was minor but she remained on sick leave for several weeks. On her return she was hostile towards me, claiming that I had done nothing to help her during the assault.

My shock and the lesson I learned that day was seeing all the prisoners standing immobile when someone to whom they were always talking was under attack. My blessing, although I did not know it then, was that the prisoners who came and stood by my office door were trying to protect me. In the prison culture, if they were not in collusion with the attackers, they would not have easily allowed anyone to disrespect them or their space by pushing them out the way to get into my office.

Lockdown. February 20.

I arrive at work prepared to go to court to testify as a witness on behalf of the library officer who had been attacked. As I climb the steps to the front entrance of the prison, I see the sign: "NO VISITORS TODAY."

"Why?" I ask the officer.

"Shakedown," she replies.

During shakedown prisoners remain in their cells while security staff do intensive search for drugs and other illegal items.

"A day without having to watch my back from prisoners is like a day in heaven," I say, grinning with utmost glee.

The officer laughs. All staff, but especially non-security staff, love a workday when there is no prisoner movement. We are more relaxed and can now work in an atmosphere without having to constantly watch our backs. In addition, when prisoners are on lockdown, except for those banging on their cell doors, the atmosphere is quiet. We, the non-security staff, can let our guards down and, if we wish, go outside the walls for lunch. Heavenly.

I enter the institution, spreading my arms and folder for the usual inspection. I collect the library keys, and exchange pleasantries with the officer on duty. Exchanges like this depend on the personality of the officer. Some of them, especially the females, are often impassive, impersonal, and abrupt to the point of being considered rude. Others are friendly, funny, and positive.

Before I descend the stairs that would lead me through the door into the yard, I pass the visiting room. None of the usual movements here.

The recreation yard is empty and quiet. From a distance, I hear the occasional rattle of the cell doors and prisoners shouting. I pass the workshop where prisoners would normally be heading to begin their daily assignment. Eerily quiet. A ghost yard, unlike other days when I walk through the yard to get the mail. Then, dozens of prisoners walk the perimeter, flexing muscles, playing basketball, exercising, lifting weights, sitting on benches talking, or just "bullshitting," as they say, laughing, making bets, and surreptitiously conducting business. Today my safe, quiet trek brings to mind the day I was doing my routine visit to the administrative offices to get the library mail.

As I walked by, one of the men sitting on the sideline said to me, "Miss, we been noticing that when you walk through this yard, you walk without any fear."

He and his buddies roared with laughter when my 5-feet-6-inch, 125-lb. body straightened, looked this hulk in the eye and growled.

"You ever try anything and I would beat up all of you."

"You don't have to worry, miss, you are safe."

"Good." I feigned a grim, fierce look, laughed, and continued on my way.

Today it is safe to leave all the library doors open and work without interruption. Officers bring in dogs who sniff every corner of each room, books, and cupboards. I breathe a sigh of relief after their search showed no illegal substances hidden in the library, especially in the rarely used hardback books that are great hiding places for drugs. If illegal substances had been found, the library would likely be subjected to continuous searches and scrutiny, possibly temporary closure, and restrictions on procuring or receiving hardback books, just like it happened in another prison, where officers found drugs hidden in a legal reference book. I am also relieved because many security staff, while not openly hostile to the library, often say that library staff is too accommodating in a place where security is paramount. Others say the library only needs legal books to satisfy constitutional mandate.

The library clerks always laugh when I tell them that if officers find contraband in the library, repercussions from me would be worse than what the authorities would have in store for them. I knew by then that they respected the library and that one among them would find ways to alert me if they saw things amiss. These clerks monitored and used their own methods to get the stolen materials back into the library. I was aware that while a lot of this was protecting the library, there was also the culture of outrage if others outside their area disrespected their territory. Of course, much depended on the clerk not being in collusion with the thief, a drug dealer or a sex partner.

Like a scene in a play, they used various techniques to provide alerts, hints, and warnings before or in anticipation certain activities.

"Ms. Shirley, that guy who always come in and keep on his coat is using it to hide books and tear out magazine pictures."

"Ms. Shirley, careful when Brown in the library and keep asking you things because him love to touch."

When I get the information, I become more watchful, while respecting the need for the safety of the informant. Sometimes I alert the officer on duty about my suspicions, never letting on it was a tip.

At the end of each normal workday, I retrace my steps heading towards the visiting room, control center, and the front entrance to return the radio and keys before exiting the building. The visiting area always has prisoners interacting with their visitors under the direct scrutiny of security staff. On this lockdown day, however, the area does not have officers overseeing prisoners, but officers overseeing confiscated items from the prison cells. Today, instead of heading towards the exit, I go inside the visiting room, curious, fascinated, amused, and amazed to see and get a closer look at the items on display. I see a square wooden box with aluminum foil pasted around the insides of the box that is approximately 12 inches high. One side is open. Inside, there are three large electric bulbs. An electric cord hangs from the side.

"What on earth is that?" I ask.

"Oh, that! They make it and use it like a microwave oven to keep the food warm when they steal from the kitchen," the officer replies. He points to four recently tailored blue denim vests that have detailed straight diamond-shaped stitches that go through various layers of padding. "How you like this?"

"If dem try escaping over the wall, the bullets won't harm them through those jackets," another officer remarks.

"But how can they do this without anyone seeing them?" I ask.

They reply that the incarcerated guys had stolen the sewing machine parts bit by bit, put them together in their cells, and did their sewing in a section of the building that has very little surveillance.

After Lockdown

Prisoners are back to their regular routine and I ask the clerks about their confiscated contraptions.

"We have to manufacture our own microwave," they reply, laughing.

They describe the many items that they cook in their cell without the knowledge of security staff. For wine making, they sneak oranges, apple, bread and anything else they find to make wine.

"How?" I ask.

"The guys who do cleanup detail carry large plastic bags and they store the wine in the bags. Sometime they give the officers some. The rest they sell to other prisoners and if they don't get pay, they punish the guy."

My informants never use the first person when they share these stories with me.

March 4

Tee hands me a large manila envelope, saying, "Your birthday. I don't know if you will be coming to work tomorrow, so I'm giving you your card now."

I open the envelope to find an elaborately made bronze card with words engraved in silver on a blue background. The words "NASCENT," "Cherubims," and "Seraphims" were written on the outer cover of the card.

"Nice," I say.

"You deserve it," he replies, adding that if I did not know what they mean, I should look up the meaning of the words "seraphim," "cherubim," and "nascent" in the dictionary.

March 5

Today is my birthday and also the birthday for Low, one of the library clerks. He sees the card from Tee and says he feels badly about giving me his very small ordinary card.

"Ever heard of the widow's mite?" I ask him.

"What's that?"

"Go ask one of your Bible-reading friends," I reply.

Later he returns and tells me that now he understands what I meant. Next day, he brings me a birthday card that I place on my desk beside Tee's.

Week of March 11

An instructor calls to say she had a car accident and would not be at work that day.

"Tell her to stay in bed on her back, she should be in for some good money." Lee laughs.

Midweek, all the library clerks sign a get-well card and ask me to get it to the instructor.

I spend a lot of my workday in the processing room, where five library clerks process new books, magazines, file clippings from newspapers and magazines, and work on legal requests, giving priority to prisoners on segregation and PC. In this work area, I overhear conversations on topics in the news, the prison, family issues, or humorous interchanges. I try not to get drawn in these discussions. Not easy to do since they constantly ask my opinion.

From the magazine desk directly across the room, Tee observes my interaction with these clerks. Sometimes he comes into the room as if looking for something but never talks or interacts with anyone. One time he said that he noticed how relaxed I am with the other guys leaving him out in spite of his being a devoted worker. Today I respond that some people try too hard to please and sometimes that in itself could be a problem in a prison environment. He stands, folding his arms in a relaxed pose as he responds.

"Maybe I try too hard."

"As I told you before, Tee, one should work and do the right thing, because of self-motivation, not solely to impress another person or for seeking to be in their good grace. I, for example, appreciate a clerk working very hard, but prefer to know that the person is doing it for himself, not to impress me, since I may not be around all the time."

"Some of those you seem to trust may not be so trustworthy," he replies.

"I am very aware of where I am and the extent to which I can trust anyone in this environment," I say.

"Your faith in those persons may not be justified," he counters with conviction. "I know much more than you."

"I am aware of much more than I let on. I make the decision to ignore the things that are not detrimental. Besides, I give each person enough time and warning, openly and subtly. I know who I can deal with. Of all the workers, I would trust only one person 90% of the time."

He cautions me about that one person, then adds if it was he, it would be funny since he would be warning against himself.

"Anyway," he states, "it could not be me, for we don't have that rapport."

"Rapport and trust are two different things in my book."

He looks puzzled. I explain that there are persons I like, and with whom I had good rapport but it did not mean that I trust them. The irony is that in spite of his fulsome ways, Tee is one of the prisoners I feel I can trust.

March 15

Low: "I would like to live in a country where one can have many wives."

"Why?"

"It must make a man feel good. Make him feel like a king," he says with a dreamy look. "One thing I must do before I die, I must go to Jamaica or an African country. It must be strange to be somewhere where all the people, teachers, and leaders are black. That must be a great feeling. Yes, my dream is to visit one of those countries."

April 5

My first day returning to work after two weeks on vacation.

"I know where you went," some prisoners say as they enter the library. "You are blacker than me. You must have been lying on the beach in Jamaica all the time. Couldn't you take me with you?"

May 29

During a few days' leave from work, I cut my shoulder-length hair to a short crop. The prisoners keep coming into the library, and as the word spread, more of them visit. Some chide me for cutting off my long lovely hair, although they say my new hairdo makes me look like a young girl, and it really looks nice. A few prisoners say they figure I have a new man since I was looking so nice of late.

June 12

I am looking at men's watch advertisements in *TIME* magazine.

"I like to see that," Lane said. "Like to see ladies looking at those. That is about three rocks."

"Rocks? What is that?"

"You don't know what a rock is? Ask Ms. N (my new assistant librarian), she should know."

"A rock," he explains, "is when you process the cocaine or crack and crystalize it." He points to one button on the telephone." One little piece like that is one rock and that is worth about one hundred dollars."

"What!" Low exclaims. "It must be expensive in your area. That piece is worth about 25 dollars."

They argue for a while on the size and cost of a piece of rock.

"What do you do with it?" My ignorance on display. "Do you melt it, and inject it, sniff it or what?"

"You put it in a pipe and light it," they explain. Low laughs. "You have to go easy, though, because it will finish too quickly."

"How long does that last?"

"About an hour."

"Then what?"

"You go find another dose."

"But that is a lot of money. Where will you get all that money?"

"You sell everything, steal, knock down everybody to get the money."

"Even the girls! You should see some girls. When they hot they even strip their clothes."

"You mean they are hot sexually or just the drugs?"

"Both sexually and otherwise."

"COUNT TIME," the officer shouts, putting an end to my street and drug education.

At the officer's shout, the clerks move towards the exit waving. One of them saying to me, "Be good now."

July 1

It is the end of the workday for the clerks. Everyone has left, except Lon and Low. They continue my education on heroin, crack and cocaine. I get information on how it is mixed and sold as well as its effect on persons, and how the trade is conducted. I believe they are more amused by my naiveté and the dumb questions I ask. Perhaps this is why one of the prisoners from the general population told me that he had never met a positive black woman like me before.

July 15: Officers as Hostages

The officer in charge of the school warns me to be cautious as word is out that there would be an escape attempt and diversions would precede this attempt. Everything appears to be normal throughout the day At home that evening, I hear on the news that two officers are being held as hostages.

July 20 - 25: Lockdown

I arrive at work. Temperature is in the 90s. Some prisoners are in tents, others are strolling around the tents, looking like Nomads, or animals in cages. Some are dirty and partially clothed since their washed clothes are hanging on makeshift clotheslines. From the dorms where they have been evacuated come chairs, tables, a television and lots of other items that will more likely be confiscated since they are contraband items taken from the prisoners' units.

Today the prison is on lockdown. An officer said they confiscated 60 gallons of wine, 10 bags of weed, and 68 packets of chips. I am not surprised because sometimes I smell alcohol on some prisoners who visit the library. On one occasion I smelled alcohol on one of my library clerks, but he just said hello, acted normally, then went to work in his assigned area. I neither asked nor said anything about the smell of alcohol, but some days later he volunteered information.

"Ah, Ms. S. You ever see how some of them inmates wear big coats? Those coats have pockets all around. So if you work in the kitchen or you have a friend who work in the kitchen, over a period you have enough bread, apple, and other things to let them ferment and get wine. We then have large garbage bags and like on New Year's Eve, we have enough to celebrate."

"Don't the officers see and confiscate those things?"

"Of course, but they don't interfere. Some of them are for sale," they laughed.

"Like the time you tried to get me to break the prison rule?" I asked one clerk.

"Ah, Ms. S. Ah really wanted to make sure I get my poem out to the radio station."

It is a violation of institution rules for staff to mail any item for prisoners. Rule violators become the prisoners' mule. Granting even one favor makes it is difficult to break continuing as the benefitting prisoner will threaten to expose "the mule" to prison administration. One day the library clerk came to me with a desperate, forlorn, and pleading look, holding out a large brown envelope as he asked me if I could do him a big favor.

"Ms. S.," he said, "you know they have this poetry competition on Channel 13. I wrote a poem and I don't want this envelope to get bent if I put it in the institutional mail. I also want to get it out on time." He came forward, stretching the envelope towards me. "Look inside, Ms. S., it has no contraband. You can even read the poem. I would really appreciate if you put it in the outside mailbox."

"So now you want me to lose my job," I retorted. "You know what you are asking me to do is against the corrections rules."

He looked sheepish, muttered something, then left with his envelope. I neither knew nor asked what happened to his poem. What I did know was that if I had mailed his letter, word would get around that I was a "mule." He and other prisoners would no doubt use this as a way to demand more favors. I also never knew whether this request was genuine or if in the collusion with others, testing my availability for rule violations.

Corrections Education Staff

Mrs. T.

After I witnessed the painful repercussions experienced by a corrections officer and Mrs. T., an educational instructor who helped two prisoners, I am glad that I never succumbed to the prisoner's plea regarding mailing his poem.

Mrs. T. was a 60-plus-year-old instructor and a quiet, kind, gentle Christian woman. She and her husband worked as missionaries overseas, and on their return to the United States she volunteered at the Baltimore City jail next door to The Pen. Her experience volunteering at the jail made her apply for a job teaching at The Pen.

One student told her he was a good friend of one of the women with whom she had worked at the jail. He told her about dire financial hardships and threats to his life from fellow prisoners to whom he was in debt. Prison rules prohibited money or gift exchange from staff, but he beseeched Mrs. T. to help save his life by giving the money to his female friend on the outside. She gave money for a while but as the requests continued, perhaps she realized she was being used, or she did not have more money to continue, or maybe she finally realized that she was in trouble for institutional rule violations. Mrs. T. told the prisoner that she would not give any more money to his friend. When his persuasive attempts did not work, he became angry and threatened to report her to the administration. This is the technique many prisoners use to get staff to continue rule violations.

During one lunchbreak, on her own initiative Mrs. T. went to the warden and confessed how she had helped this individual who convinced her his life was in danger. We, the staff in the education building, had no prior knowledge of any of this action, so we were shocked when a corrections officer came to the building and asked one instructor to clear out Mrs. T.'s desk because she would not be allowed back in the prison. The salacious prison gossip had it that sex was involved. I never believed that, neither did the education staff.

Feeling sympathy for her, especially in light of all the rumors that were circulating, I got her address and sent her a note wishing her well. She responded:

May 1, 1989
Dear Ms Shirley

Thank you so much for your thoughtful note last week. I really needed that touch of kindness at a time when my whole world seemed upside down.

I guess I am going through the stages of grief. I have cried and prayed and talked, and try to keep busy. My worst time is in the early morning when my mind wants to go back and figure it all out—instead of moving forward.

I made the mistake of calling into school last week. It was too soon. The wound was too fresh, and I lost some ground I have gained.

Then yesterday (Sunday) a lady at church told me she had heard an ugly rumor and again the wound was opened. I did get a chance then to talk to my young pastor—a very kind and compassionate man, and he assured me I could do nothing about rumors and I must not assume guilt when I knew I had done the best I knew under the circumstances.

I hurt for my students who are no doubt hearing many things and wondering where the truth lies. If opportunity arise, assure them that I am the same person I have always been, and the same person they knew me to be; I had a problem I could not solve except by leaving. I miss them a lot.

After a while, I hope a very good teacher will be found who will just as energetically lead my students towards getting their G.E.D. Let my friends know, if you have the opportunity, that I will be all right after a while. The healing will take some time, of course, so I will just be at home here catching up on housework etc. and doing some writing.

My family have been supportive and my daughter has amazed me with her strength and wise words when I have shared thing with her. I don't know what I would do without her.

The book of Psalms has been a comfort to me, especially Ps. 30-37 & Ps. 91. Then I remember too how David failed, and Peter failed, but God forgave and restored and reinstated. Those thoughts give me comfort.

Perhaps some time later I will call you when I am feeling better.

Thanks for your prayers and good wishes. They helped a lot.

God bless you and give you strength for your busy days.

Love.

T

The other staff incident involved exchanges between a prisoner in the segregation unit and a female officer who worked in that section. The officer had done several favors for the prisoner. When his demands increased, she decided to discontinue. He threatened to expose her. During their verbal exchange, he turned on a tape, recorded their conversation where he deliberately mentioned some things she had done for him previously. He gave the recording to another corrections staff. The officer was suspended pending investigations.

Mrs. J.

Who is Mrs. J. that Cal mentioned in one of his letters to me? She was the new full-time librarian I hired to work with me after I received funding to extend library services to the other prisons that were within a block of the penitentiary. Baltimore Pre-Release Unit (BPRU), Baltimore City Correctional Center (BCCC), MRDCC, and the recently constructed Supermax. These were various levels (maximum to prerelease) of state prisons supervised by The Department of Public Safety and Corrections (DPSCS). Hiring another librarian also enabled some evening services to prisoners who worked during the daytime.

The presence of a new female staff anywhere in the prison often results in an influx of prisoners who find creative ways to justify their need to be in that work area. In the library, while some visitors claimed they were seeking information, it was clear that many of them visited more to gawk, study, analyze, and assess than to seek genuine information. "Getting to know you" by asking a variety of questions seemingly related to legal or reader's advisory needs.

Unlike my skinny physique, Mrs. J. was well endowed. The men's eyes followed her every movement. A few months after her arrival, one clerk said to me, "Ms. Shirley, we notice that the guys want to see when Ms. J. walk so they wait till she is on the opposite side of the room, before they ask a question. Then they stay behind and watch her walk across the room to the reference desk."

"Thanks," I said.

Aware that sometimes prisoners played one staff member against the other, I was careful how I approached her. The men may have also told her things about me as well. I repeated the prisoners' comments, adding that in public, special, or academic libraries, it was the norm to accompany the users to help them find what they were seeking. The prison atmosphere, however, often require alternative strategies.

"The prison library is a different setting. It's not that we are giving less service. The men are here for a long time, and except for someone who has a specific court date, there is not a great deal of urgency. It is best to direct them to the reference desk where there are prison library clerks who have more knowledge of legal reference than you and I. They can also write down their request and we will aim to provide the answer by the next day. We can get their court dates and give priority to those persons with specific dates," I said. I also reminded her that the Maryland Correctional librarians do not give legal advice and our prison library is not a law library.

One day a clerk came to me and said, "Ms. S., please tell Mrs. J. to be careful how she sit at the circulation desk because some of them crazy prisoners, instead of putting the books they return on the circulation desk, or just putting it in the return slot, them bend down to look in the slot."

"What's wrong with that?" I asked, thinking the user was just ensuring the book got in the slot.

"If she sitting on the high stool by the circulation desk, wearing a dress, and they peep, they may get lucky and see something."

Another day, from the library entrance, a prisoner shouted to his companion on the inside, "Hey, bro, Ms. J. have on a jacket?"

"Yeah," was the response.

"Ah, man, I not coming to the library then."

Apparently, wearing a jacket hid too much of her mammary projections for this potential user. As a supervisor, my goal was to show high statistics for circulation or visits. Should I tell Mrs. J. that the library's circulation or visits increased when she did not wear a jacket? I merely repeated the prisoner's comment in order to help create more awareness for her.

I tried mentoring Mrs. J. but the constant skillful manipulative nature of the prison atmosphere made it tough for me to be observing or correcting everything, while at the same time watching my back and running the libraries. I also tried to be careful since I knew they played one staff against the other.

About six months after her arrival, two library clerks said to me, "Ms. S., the guys are saying they noticed how Ms. J. change her dress style. She looking more flashy nowadays and have new hairdo. They saying she must be trying to impress somebody."

Another library worker, a very good-looking, charming, full-of-himself prisoner, was constantly trying to get her attention. I had noticed, so did the prison clerks. I don't recall how long she stayed at The Pen, but one day, I was surprised when she laughingly said to me, "I am leaving to work in a state psychiatric library, where the residents are under heavy medication and doped up. I know I can control that situation better than this one, where the prisoners are constantly finding ways to manipulate."

I respected her wisdom and practicality in doing a self-analysis and moving on, based on her assessment.

Prisoners

Marlo September 1990

Marlo, the new library clerk, had pearly white even teeth, a disarming smile, and very dark skin. Everyone called him "Blackie." Several months after he began working in the library, during one of our conversations, I told him the name "Blackie" was derogatory and he should not accept it. After this, I never heard anyone address him except by his nickname, Mo. He was very bright, learned very quickly and I did not have to spend much time teaching him library duties. He lacked self-discipline, however, easily influenced by others. It seems he could not say no to those who constantly asked him for favors. He never stayed on task, and disappeared from his post frequently. I spent a lot of time asking the education officer to locate him.

I should have fired Mo after the first instances of unauthorized absences, or based on my suspicion that he may be absconding with some of the library books, but I kept giving him breaks. This may have conveyed weakness on my part, providing him with incentives for more deviant actions. The day I decided I had had enough of his uncooperative behavior, I wrote him a "Ticket," which could result in a setback on his record. News spread that I had written Mo a Ticket. He confronted me with anger and hostility, demanding to know why I had done this to him since it may mean an additional 18 months' stay at

The Penitentiary. He said that he did not want to work in the library anymore. I let him go. Three weeks passed. One day I looked up and saw Mo standing by the circulation desk with his usual disarming smile. Hostility gone. He asked to speak to me.

"I have been reflecting, I know I have done wrong, and went to see my case manager. I saw your statement about my hostility. That hurt me very much because it was not my intention. Although your actions were unjustified, I would not like you to consider me hostile. I am here to apologize and hope you are not still angry with me," he said.

"As far as I am concerned," I replied, "the matter is closed. I find it unfortunate that you do not want to accept the consequences of your behavior. If you intend to return and function normally and successfully in society, there are rules to which you must adhere. Many of these rules you will not like, some you will find stupid and pointless, but compliance may make the difference between your remaining in the society or returning to prison."

He listened, signaled his agreement, then asked me about my workforce.

"Not good," I responded, knowing that he was fully aware of this. He offered to do volunteer service as "penance." It was time for him to return to his cell, so I neither gave him an answer nor rehired him.

Years later, after I left and returned to the prison environment as Library Coordinator, Mo was one of the volunteers for "Family Literacy @ Your Library,"[8] a program I initiated where prisoners read to and with their children. He became an enthusiastic, excellent participant, and program facilitator in this program that received many accolades in Maryland and from other prisons across the country.

---

[8] Reflections on Family Literacy @ a Prison Library. http://olos.ala.org/columns /?p=121.

Nate

Nate was quiet, polite, neatly dressed, always with a thoughtful expression. He looked like a teenager. An older prisoner who became his mentor took him to the library, encouraging him to use it to seek information, then later to apply for a job. On the mentor's recommendation I hired Nate as a library clerk. I also became a sort of mentor to him and was surprised when he was implicated in the 1988 prison riot. He was confined to Supermax, the lockdown prison designed for the most violent offenders. In that area, prisoners were locked in their cells for 23 hours, allowed only one hour outside, in a small confined area. Institutional mail was their only outlet to seek and receive library information. On his release from Supermax, Nate returned to work in the library. I cautioned him about the people he chose as friends.

"They really harassing me for the past few weeks, Ms. Shirley," he said.

"Drugs?" I asked.

He nodded affirmatively.

"They keep calling me up on the level and keep testing my urine, and searching my cell. It is like there is no end. I think administration is really out to get me." He sounded dejected and sad.

"Could it be the company you are keeping? For your own peace of mind and tough as it may be, you may have to remove yourself from some of those 'friends' you have here."

He listened with the usual quiet respect. Maybe my advice had some impact, because to my knowledge, he never got in trouble up to the time I left The Pen. Years later, as I made quarterly visits to the prisons, I saw Nate on the Eastern shore, and in Hagerstown, both lesser security prisons to which he had been transferred. He asked me about introducing the family literacy program in those areas, as he had heard other prisoners talk positively about the program in Jessup.

Letters from Nate

6/6/95

Mrs. Shirley

First of all, I sincerely trust and hope that you're well as can be.

I realize this may come as a complete surprise to you. So therefore don't be so taken back. O.K. (smile)

Believe me, I always intended or wanted to write. It just seems I never got around to doing so. Forgive me because there's really no excuse however, I always thought of you and your wellbeing. And at many times I did inquire about you through Mrs. Newman. So, you see, I never did actually forget about you. I guess thoughts counts, nuh (smile). Sincerely speaking my mind was indeed obsessed with the memory of you. And I just hope you're well!

Anyway I wanted to let you know that I finally transferred. Regardless of my circumstances, I really did enjoy meeting someone like you as well as having the opportunity to work along with you and Mrs. Newman. Believe me Mrs. Shirley, it honestly made a difference. And I want to thank you for that. Its been good! I missed you__

Take good care!

A Friend

Nate

**Ms Shirley

To be honest, it just hit me exactly how much time we've spent shared and worked together. Well, actually the time that I did work for that matter (smile)

I know at times I was a pain with my running in and out from my job post. But you always let it past or so I thought. I'm sorry for them particular times.

Nevertheless let me say that I've really enjoyed working for you. I really appreciated your being you. A friend at times, a mother figure at times, and of course the other categories I'll cherish as my personal secret thoughts.

It's been fun Ms Shirley. Take it easy, be safe, and don't forget to drop by whenever circumstances allow.

Oh by the way, it's been a real pleasure every single day. I truly mean that (smile)

Take care.
Nate

**Nate: 14 Sept. 1995

It certainly was real good hearing from you.

Plus you'll be glad to know that I have taken advantage of opportunities here.

In fact I've obtained a library clerk position here, and of course it's in the legal reference.

I wouldn't have it no other way

Thanks again
Take Care
Nate

**Nate: Jan. 23, 1996
Dear Ms Shirley

First, I sincerely hope that my letter receives you well. I'm alright here. I guess, hanging in there, under the circumstances.

My reason for writing is, I wonder if I may have a character reference from you. To be placed inside my base file. Considering you were in fact, my employer for awhile.

You see, next month, February, I go in front of the Parole Board. My very first consideration in fact. But to be honest, I'm not really expecting any great outcomes. Considering the state of lifers at present. However, I would very much appreciate a letter of character from you. If that at all seems appropriate. Let me know nevertheless OK. Take care—

Nate

**Nate: 12/28/97
Dear Ms Shirley

I received your card well. And it was good hearing from you. Things are as good as they can possibly be with me here—

I really meant to write you sooner to let you know how things went on, my parole hearing. Not so good or what I really anticipated.

Anyway, although I guess it could've been much worse. Still I keep optimistic that re-release will one day be reinstated. I assume eventually it'll come to be in the near future. My Wish_____

Regardless, I try to keep things in its proper perspective. I tend to be realistic about things but more importantly, level minded! What can I say, Only that I'll never lose focus!

Well, I did finally get my Case back in the Courts. Wish me well.

You take care OK
Hope your Holidays
Are pleasant.

My Response to Nate's Request for Character Reference in Feb. 1996

To: Whom it may concern
RE: Nate

While I was Regional Librarian and Supervisor of the Correctional Education Libraries located in Baltimore, Maryland, Mr. N. worked as a clerk in the Penitentiary Library.

During the time he worked with me, he was courteous, punctual and had good relations with both prisoners and staff.

Mr. Nate enrolled in the Educational programs in

order to improve himself and to better prepare himself for future undertakings.

All the above qualities augur well for Mr. Nate in any future turn his life may take.

GLS

Horace

To ensure equal access to prisoners on protective custody (PC) and administrative segregation (SEG), I distributed fliers informing residents how to use institutional mail to seek library information. Once a week either a library clerk or the librarian visit the units with a cart of popular reading and legal materials. Due to the propensity to use this position as media for drug trade or deals including trading library materials for favors, finding a clerk to work in these areas was difficult. On a visit to PC, I met Horace, who volunteered to distribute the newspapers in the unit. I knew nothing about him, so did not follow up on his offer. After his release from PC, he applied to be a library clerk and I hired him.

He was restless, never remained in one spot for long, and I found myself constantly berating him for his immaturity.

"I don't have a good day if you don't holler at me," he told me one day.

I realized then that he deliberately left his post in order to have me search for and fuss with him. He was unfazed when I attacked his immaturity. I tried ignoring him for long spells, but in order to get the work done properly and supervise him, there had to be some interaction. Eventually Horace settled down. Somewhat. He disappeared less frequently and his work improved. By then, he had become my favorite person "on whom to pick." I teased him, fussed with him, and he took it all with good humor.

In the prison system, case managers handle prisoners' cases, recommending them for jobs or for transfer to lesser-security prisons. Rumor was rife that a certain case manager was gay and the clerks regaled me with stories about his affairs with some of the incarcerated men. This manager frequently called the library, requesting Horace to his office. Horace laughed when, with a smirk, I referred to this manager as "your friend."

"I want to get out of the penitentiary, Ms. Shirley," he would respond. Sometimes he took one look at my face and hurried in the opposite direction, saying, "Time for me to go, Miss Shirley, 'cause I know what you going to say now."

The day he came to work wearing a black beret and took it off to display a cleanshaven head. I looked at him in disbelief, then started to laugh, telling him that there is no way I could have a serious conversation with him while his head looked like that. When Horace left The Pen, so did my source of juicy prison gossip.

Horace's Letters

Horace xx Prisoners#
Hagerstown MD
October 23, 1990
Hello Ms Shirley

Hope this letter fines you in the very best of health and spirits. But due to your working situation I'll have to settle for one out of the two, and that's your health. Maybe this letter will lift your spirits, because writing you lift mine.

I first want to thank you for allowing me the opportunity to have worked for you. I can truly say that I'm going to miss you, because its very hard to meet positive people in situations such as this. What I've learned from you will stay with me for the rest of my life, because it allowed me to see that I can accomplish anything in life I want if I aggressive. Thank you Ms. Shirley.

So far, everything here is okay. Its much more controlable and orderly than the Pen. But I guess the reason for that is they have a lot of young people here, and people coming and going.

I haven't been to the library yet, like you said, its kind of hard here. But if there's a will, there's a way. I did write the librarian, so far I haven't heard anything. If I don't hear from her by the end of the week, I'll write her again.

I've seen a few people here I know, but I haven't had the opportunity to talk with them yet concerning the programs. I have seen or heard of the drug program here something the Parole Board want me to get involved in. I'll have to wait awhile for the college programs, because I'll have to get a grant or something.

I've seen Jack one time sense I have been here, and he seems not to want to talk. But that's okay, who needs friends like that.

So how's things going with you. I know you glad you don't have me around to bug you. But your wrong about that. I do have stamps and the Pen Address. But my main goes (goals?) are to let you know how I'm doing, and what I'm doing. Because keeping in contact with positive people, makes me do positive things. Plus I know your not going to allow me to get lazy or mess up.

How's Ms N? Tell her hello for me. And also tell her that I'm not going to allow anyone else to call me a Fool or … but her.

Tell Big Low I'll write him soon, and to take care. You have a very good worker in "Low", pretty soon he'll be running the library. I wish nothing but the best for him.

As for you Ms Lady, you had better take care of yourself, and I mean that!!! Don't' tell me not to worry about you, because I always worry about friends, in which I only have a few.

I'll write you soon and I will stay out of trouble and do the things that would allow me my freedom. Just don't cut me off.   A Friend For Life. Horace.

January 4, 1991
Hello Ms Shirley

Hope this letter fines you in the very best of health and spirits. Since the last time you heard from me things have gotten pretty busy. Yet I haven't forgotten you. I did receive your card in which brighten my day.

I wasn't able to get a job in the library (and I'm kind of glad about that). The Librarian in this location seems to have a racial problem, and working for her would have caused me a lot of problems.

Guess what? I have a job as a Teachers Aid! Now you know how my English is and I haven't past a English class when I was in college. So far things are working out pretty good, yet I'm not looking forward to the time when I really have to work with someone.

Since the last you heard from me, I was moved to an open housing unit, in which they say is a honor unit. I do have a key to my cell, and that takes a lot of getting used too. But I can't get use to these white officers making racial statements and disrespecting me. But I guess this is a test from God to give me strength when I get my freedom.

Locksley is on the same unit, and not working. Since he got here, I haven't did much of anything. But he has been getting visits from his funny friend.

No, No. I haven't heard from that so call person you thought or think is my friend. I guess he found someone else.

So hows the workers, especially Big Low? Tell him I said hello and I'll write him soon. I did get a letter from…-Bey a few weeks back, but he didn't say much of anything.

Please tell Ms N. that I said hello, and I'm no longer a prisoner. I'm, a Teachers Aid.

Ms Shirley, you take care of yourself. I will keep in touch, and continue to use the skills and motivational words you gave me.

Always a Friend
Horace .

Ronnie, 1988

When I interviewed Ronnie for the library clerk position, he did not impress me, I gave him the job because of high recommendations from another library clerk. He worked well, but was crude and loud, unlike the other workers. Sometimes the clerks invited me into the workroom to requests little perks. I listened, but for the most part did not agree to any of their demands. My objective was to try and conform to administrative guidelines, and to help them prepare for a successful return to society. The week after he started working, Ronnie became the most vocal among the library clerks.

"Ms. Shirley, since we don't get much pay and we have to work so hard, maybe some days we could just come in to work, sign in and then go away."

"No way," I said. "This setting is preparing you for the work world in case you return to society. Behave like that outside, and you would not only lose your job, but may cause someone else to lose theirs."

As the months went by Ronnie became less vocal. He continued working but I got the impression that he lacked motivation. One area of consistency was his questions on a variety of topics. No matter the subject, I took the time to answer as honestly as I knew how. He listened with an intensity, giving the impression he was digesting every word. Whenever he questioned my decisions in an accusatory, brusque, and somewhat rude manner, I ignored him. I realized later that he was not intentionally being offensive. He came to prison from the streets at age 16. He has been incarcerated for 8 years. His manners and outlook were based on his perception of his needs for survival. This meant acting "baad" to earn respect from cohorts in a setting where respect is often earned by the magnitude of an offense or rule violation. Some prisoners gained respect and reputation by fighting, cursing, hurting someone, not letting anyone take any liberties with them.

One morning, Ronnie came to me saying he wanted to discuss something. He said that the previous evening, he attended a function with many outside visitors. He knew he was capable of answering the questions that the visitors posed, but he did not answer much. He said he just used single-word responses and knew they thought he was not very intelligent, he had really wanted to make a good impression. He concluded by saying that he felt badly about being so nonverbal. I searched for and lent him a few books on building self-confidence, how to talk to people, and how to sell yourself. I have no idea whether he read them.

For Martin Luther King's birthday, I asked library users to write their impressions of Dr. King and what he meant to them. I promised I would have some of them read their essays at a program I was planning. Ronnie came to me saying that he would try to write an essay because he became interested in Dr. King after he came to prison. He stated that he learned things about Dr. King that he never knew before and he has developed "a healthy respect for the man." During the program when the men read their essays, Ronnie told me that he started but had not completed his essay as he realized it was in part due to his lack of self-discipline. Sensing that he really wanted to read what he had written, and remembering our previous conversations, I told him he could participate by sharing his feelings and impressions on Dr. King. He perked up, happy to speak in front of the audience. As his speech progressed, profanities crept in. Later, I commended him on his courage to speak in front of the group, then said that that his presentation was good, spoilt only by his use of profanities.

"That," I said, "is not in keeping with what Dr. King was about."

His friend who recommended him for the library position agreed with me. Next day, Ronnie sent a letter to all the members of staff who attended the gathering. He apologized for using profanities, promising to improve himself.

When Ronnie knew that he was due for transfer to another prison one morning as he arrived at work, he came to my office.

"I know you are about to leave for a meeting but I want to just take a few minutes of your time," he said.

Without any invitation, he pulled a chair and sat down, eased himself backwards in a relaxed pose, the customary stance that tells onlookers, "I have the privilege of chatting with my friend." He began to talk.

"I will soon be leaving here, Miss S. I may go any moment so I want to let you know before I leave. The last eight months that I have worked with you have been the most meaningful of my entire stay of eight-plus years in this institution. You are a professional person, you work hard and a lot of people have a lot of respect for you. I want to thank you for the experience and for imparting to me the things you did. I will carry them with me wherever I go and always."

Ronnie's Letters

13 March 1989

Greetings Mrs. Shirley

I would have written long before now, but the situation here has been pretty hectic until recently. I'm just beginning to settle down. In terms of management control and races, the prison is pretty much the same as Cal explained about the place he's at. But I'm adjusting pretty quickly. I was fortunate to get a single cell here, and I've just recently been classified to the Educ. Dept.

as a teacher's aide—that is only until space becomes available in one of the shops.

I had originally planned to work in the library but after visiting once, I decided against it. The lighting is very terrible and there furniture and equipment looks very old. Besides, after working alongside you, Howie, Mrs. J, Nate, and Cal, working here would be more of a job than a position.

Another thing about the library, it's not accessible to the prisoners. We are required to put in appointment slips, request slips, and are called, depending upon when space is available.

The population is very young in age and more so in behavior. The average age is 22. The police have absolute and total control. In fact the fear among the prisoners of the police is frightening in itself. However, there was a homicide here last week. Prisoners killing prisoners. Disgusting! Only 22 years old too.

Personally, I've been maintaining a low profile and thus far have been treated with respect and individual consideration from the officials and the prisoners. I am determined not to "allow" myself to lose sight of my objectives or get caught up with personalities of the environment.

My goal is to get out of prison! I will be moving to all honorary housing unit next week. It has a certain prestigious attachment.

To get there everyone is required to earn their way through some kind of special program, shop, school, good behavior, boot licking or what have you. Apparently, my penitentiary record qualifies me. We are rewarded a number of privileges the remaining population don't have—

phone calls, extended recreation, longer visits & less supervision, all-in-all, it's a much better housing unit in general. The guys there are more mature, more positive, and less inclined to mind other people's business. I can't wait to get there

I'm in pretty good spirits these days. I hope you are not disappointed that I did not write sooner. You are by far one of my favorite people. I heard from CAL twice. He's fine. He said he wrote you. Have you been able to see Nate yet?

I truly believe I'm going to progress through and out of this system quickly. I'm more secure of myself; meaning I understand my strengths weaknesses and limitations. The "little" talks we use to have had a lot to do with it.

Tell me what's happening down there. How is your new staff? Have you found a replacement for Mrs. J? How much longer do you think you will be there? You will keep in touch? Won't you??

After all we do have an agreement. You're supposed to be helping arrange my trip to your country. Actually, I'm thinking escort but didn't want to put it that way. I'm hoping JM and Chris will be able to join us. It would surely be a memorable occasion-Holiday!

I'm going to begin saving for it soon as I get out. Incidentally what did you think of the reference letter I revised?

If you should hear from Mrs. J, give her my best regards and say hello to Howie for me.

Tell him how I think he will like it up here. Despite its bad points the programs are geared to put guys back on the streets- if they believe you deserve it. I'm very optimistic.

Take care yourself & write when you can. Be safe

Ronnie

PS. I received your message from John M.

31 March '89

Greetings Ms Shirley

How is everything down there? I heard from JM tonight and he said you were disappointed you had not heard from me. I am sorry to hear that. I had written you a couple weeks ago and thought you received my letter. I didn't write before then because wanted to wait until I had something positive to relay. I "hated" this place the first few weeks. I'm okay now. I've since settled down and began working my way through the system. The racism and arrogance is just as you and Chris prepared me for.

I did not apply for a position in the library. After working for/with you under such pleasant conditions, doing the "same work" here would be more of a job because the conditions aren't nearly the same. For one thing, there is no "you" to make the difference. I'm working evenings as a teacher's aide (math)I'm really sorry that you did not get my first letter. I asked JM to emphasize the point in case you don't receive this one either. I think of you often and one of the things I miss most at the "Pen" is you and the wisdom I'd get from our conversations. Excluding the staff, this is a immature and ignorant population.

In comparison to the Pen, there is no apparent advantage in being here. It depends on how you look at it. The forced discipline and imaginative ways to maintain a healthy attitude, inspite it all, are good lessons to learn. The one good thing about this place, unlike the Pen, is guys leave here and go directly home every single day of the week. There is not a spirit of hopelessness here as it is at the Pen. I'd like to know how you are doing and how much longer you may be there. Please stay in touch. I'm hoping to visit your country with you one day.

Have you seen Nate yet? If when you next hear from Mrs. J. say hello for me. Also say something nice to Howie for me. It's been great having the experience to work for/with you. Do be safe. Okay.

Yours truly. Ronnie

Damon

In the reading area when prisoners visit the library, I say hello and sometimes exchange pleasantries. Many of them try to get my attention by asking what appears to be genuine questions, at times complimenting me, or commenting on some event on the news or in the prison. They tell me that in this dismal, forbidding place, I represent a breath of fresh air. I always respond by saying that as long as they did not try to get personal, I would continue to be whom they see.

One morning Damon handed me a note. I was busy and put it aside. Later he asked if I had read it, I said no, but assured him that when I had a spare minute, I would. True to my words, I searched for it, and read the contents below.

Dear Shirley

Hello I know this might seem surprise. Don't get the wrong impression but I only wanted to get something straight. I kind of lie to you about me the only reasons I make out bursts is because I'm in here for hurting someone I really love that's why I do some of the things I do. It was a mistake and it's really hurting me inside. I know you understand. Don't think I am not good at heart because I am. It was one of those relationship were one being truthful and the other cheating. Please understand don't get mad at me for writing this note, its just I feel like now that I know I trust you, also you always listen even if I clown at time. ok. This is what I wanted to talk to you about, I try not to lie anymore. Thank you Shirley. Now place ... this in the trash. Again don't get mad. I mean no harm nor am I try to get fresh. Thanks Again be seeing you later.

Dear Shirley

Hello. Hope you had a wonderful (Mother's Day). As for me, I am doing okay. Except I have slight problem and it happens to be you.

Why haven't you been communicating with me? I know this isn't something mandatory, but as I stated a while back, I enjoy talking with you. By listening to you it motivates me to strive on and look forward to a better day.

When I told you about my situation I was only being honest with you. I know I didn't to but I was only letting you know why I really act up or make certain out bursts. It really gets to me at times, but I got to continue to maintain my sanity because this was someone I truly care for and love. Now I don't want you to look at me as someone who's nice or funny but rather as a young man with a wonderful personality.

I'm very talent easy going with so many good qualities. So please continue to talk with me or not shy away or anything of that nature. Like I said I enjoy you as a person. I like you because you are yourself and you always speak to me in RESPECTFUL MANNER. Take care. Talk to you later. Again hope your Mother's day a successful day. And look forward to more of them. Bye: You are a very special Mother too. Even though I don't know you.

After Reading. Please Place In Waste Can!

I hired Damon as a library sanitation clerk. It was obvious that this lifted his self-esteem, and in his gratitude he became almost fawning in his efforts to please. Sometimes I became impatient but did not have the heart to tell him to "Gimme me a break." That would hurt his feelings, especially since he had recently mentioned he thought I was ignoring him. Working in the prison showed me the fragility of the self-esteem of majority of these men, who act so tough. I learned that a thoughtless word or action, no matter how unintentional, may be misinterpreted as something done to hurt their feelings or to demean them.

Seated at my office desk one morning, Damon came to the office door and stood waiting for me to acknowledge his presence. Like all the other prisoners, he posed so that anyone on the outside watching would see that he had status or privilege to be in my office. The posture said, "Watch me, man, I can go in and talk to her and get her attention."

"Hi," I said. "What's the problem now?"

My desk was stacked and I wanted to get on with clearing out the files. I hoped he would not stay long. I was just lowering my eyes towards my desk, signaling that he was dismissed, when he said, "You dismissing me already? I just step in here and I need more time."

The way he said it made me laugh. In a flash, he sat in the chair by my desk, relaxing, aware of those on the outside were watching. The show ended when he began to talk.

"I never liked my mother."

"Why?"

"Because of what she did to us."

I remained silent.

"There were 12 of us and she would leave us in the house for a whole day in the cold, without food, and without much shelter. Sometimes she would not return till the next day. My sisters and I grew up in foster homes. I spent about 12 years in foster homes.

"I had to steal for myself and them when we were hungry. At first all I did was steal, but later I started to lie. Lying and stealing was all I knew to do. I loved my sisters. They are the only persons in the world I care about, but I watched them raped by the foster parent and later by my older brother. Honest, I was going to kill him. I went to jail for two years because I stabbed a guy who hurt my sister, then I did not care.

"I set up a plan to kill my brother and it was really a good plan, but I got here instead. Later on I started on drugs. It gave me good money. I bought cars, had a nice place and really lived well.

"An older woman I lived with tried to get me straight. She tried to get me off drugs and even to get me to go to school, but I did not listen."

He paused. I kept looking at him.

He continued. "I have a lot of things on my mind. Sometimes I just think about all the things that happen to me, and it's like my head is not on right. I think my sister is okay, though. You know, I never talk to my mother and it is only since I am in this place that I talk to her. She comes to look for me. I understand in a way why she did what she did, but I still feel resentment. I think she feels guilty and is trying to make up, though, because I hear she is looking after some children. When my sister visited and told me she was looking after some cousin's child, all I could say was, 'She can look after other people's children, but she couldn't look after us, though.'

"Now I just keep to myself and I read my Bible a lot and I am trying to pass my GED. It's hard to concentrate, though. Sometimes my mind just goes blank and nothing can penetrate. I don't know if the drugs I used to take affected me, or it's just the problems I am thinking about."

He stopped swiveling around in the chair, and looked at me.

"That is between you and me, because I never really talk to anyone so much."

"And now," I said, "get out of my office so I can do some work."

He laughed. "My therapy session is over. Tomorrow I'll come back for some more."

I bent my head and continued to work on the file I had opened before he came into my office.

Months later he was reassigned to another area as he was getting too close to staff in the education building, not acceptable in the prison environment. After that I saw him occasionally.

When I announced that I was leaving The Pen, Damon sent the note below.

942 Forrest ST. Baltimore, MD 21201

Understand this young lady, I would prefer for you to at least write at least once or twice a week. Good luck and I wish you the best in whatever you try to accomplish. So whatever you do, write me now. Don't get out there and go crazy. And then again I just say I will miss you.

Date of birth

12-17-62

954 Forrest St.

January 11, 1995

Dear Shirley

With this message comes my trust in which it is sent—a spirit of friendship.

To begin this notation, I would like to say that you are truly mis and most of all I mis-you. And to be honest there are things I wish to elaborate on, but I will refrain from speaking on them because I sometimes forget the professional part of certain things, people, places and knowing my position and opp's where I stand and that's on a convict level so I will stay within the boundary of both yours and my position.

It's a great honor to first have known you & second to be able to write, now that's a blessing by itself. I ask Mrs. NB. for your address you didn't mine. She's doing a wonderful job here, but and times I see her and she looks tired maybe she's overworking herself.

And times when I get free, times from the Paint Shop and come to say hi or look around but there are times I hesitate to speak maybe just a little shy.

Well enough talk about me. What's going on with you? Are you planning to stick with this career or move on to better things? Are you taking care of yourself? If I'm getting a little too personal, I apologize, just trying to make conversation. I also wanted you to know I achieve my GED and I'm still happy that I did it and honestly, because my reason for not really getting it sooner was having doubt, because my father use to tell me I would never get it or be nothing. Today I can honestly say I'm somebody and I am special. And I also learnt to turn my nevers into something. Hope to go to college because that would be a tremendous step in my life. I know it's a little more harder, but I'm willing to try.

I'm going to forward you a copy also.

I know you are proud of me despite the short period together, and I kind of mis seeing and working around you. Also thanks for your encourage and having confidence in me. It MEAN a lot. Well next time you speak with Ms NB. tell her to be nice to me (smile). She's a good person. My day consist of working—working out and running my organization which is General Support Group. We sponsor schools close to Murray elementary, families etc. Now preparing to write to the courts and try to get a time cut on something. Staying out of trouble, church and walk alone at all times.

Well take care If I don't' receive a response you always remember you are in my prayers and thoughts. And I truly wish you all the best. Remember Jesus loves you and so do I. Bye my friend. God Bless you

Ms Shirley and family
PS. As soon as I get some pictures I will send you one Okay? Hopes it's okay.
From Your Friend Always. Damon

Low

Low was one of the more mature prisoners. Father of a teenage son. He told me about his difficulty trying to be a good father from prison. He said he talked to his son over the telephone, but did not get the impression the son was listening. He was worried that this child would get in trouble and also become a teenage parent. Our conversations helped me with collection building. I added books on parenting from a distance, and how to talk to children about sex.
Low always gave me a card for my birthday. One year I forgot it was my birthday, until he and the clerks came in with birthday cards, wishing me happy birthday. He still sent me cards after I left the prison system.

The prison administration allowed incarcerated men to have small plants in their cells. One day Lowell brought a small plant and placed it on a shelf in my office. Weeks later, he entered my office and poured water on the plant.

"Ms. Shirley, you not taking care of the plant, you allowing it to die. I can't bear to see anything die, Ms. Shirley," he said.

I looked at him, surprised at the comment from a man who is in prison for armed robbery that resulted in a death. I don't recall my response. Only his.

"The neighborhood we come from was not a good neighborhood. Many of us didn't have any role model, so we guys try to act tough. We would steal, and buy nice things. I never hurt anybody. One night as we go into the store, we never expect to see anybody inside, but a man was there and it scared us. I had a gun and because I got scared, my hand was shaking, and ah pull the trigger. I was still scared. Ms. Shirley, ah never intend to kill anybody. Now I praying the price and ma son growing up without a father."

Low's Cards
1989

I really feel lucky … getting to work with someone who
has turned out to be such a good friend

***

Because you mean a lot
To me
Because you're on my mind
So much,
I had to set aside some time
To keep you close…
To stay in touch
Lord is always there
To Guide us through the years,
He will always comfort
And wipe away our tears…
His love is always faithful
And never untrue
His love is overflowing

Like the sun shining through.
There's no greater blessing
Than an understanding friend
One who's always bringing joy
And on whom we can depend—
There is no greater blessing
Than a friend who's loyal
And true—
The very kind of friend
That I have found in you
Happy Birthday

Love Always
A Friend to a Friend

Handmade cards after I left The Penitentiary, 1992

Happy birthday
It's so hard to forgot you
On this very special day,
Because you have touched
My life in a very special way.
It's an honor for me to
Wish you a very
Happy birthday
Love & happiness
LOW

Happy Birthday to Shirley

A Very Special Friend
It's an everyday thing with you
To care about other people
To pay attention
To what they have to say
And how they feel...
It's an everyday thing with you
To be a very kind
And loving person
And that's why
On special days like this one,
You're thought about warmly
And wished so much happiness
Wishing love and happiness
And every blessing, too,
For such a special friend
As wonderful as you.
And may you know
God's deepest joys
For you in every way,
And may they truly be a part
Of you on your birthday. Always

1994

Special Belated Birthday Wishes
To Ms. Shirley
Sending a special

Birthday "Hello"

To make you smile

And to let you know

You're thought of

In the warmest way—

God Bless you. On your special day

Dave

Dave was a very reliable library clerk. Like many of the other prisoners, he observed me a long time before I gained his trust to the point where he would share information regarding my safety and also give me information about other prisoners. He was particularly careful because he was one of the European Americans minority in the prison, and he did not have the bulk or height of many of the prisoners. From where he sat in the corner of the processing room, he saw the book thieves hiding the pilfered items in their coats. His alert:

"You might want to check out that guy."

I never acted immediately after I received this kind of information as it would be obvious who the "snitch" was. I would walk around the library as if doing a general check, then walk casually outside to the foyer and alert the officer on duty. When Dave heard that I lived in Howard County, he said he used to hang out in the Columbia Mall and sell dope.

"But you know because I'm white nobody suspect anything."

When I said I like to walk along the Columbia pathways, he cautioned.

"Watch out when you go through the walk path alone, sometimes the criminals look out for single females, so it better if you walk with somebody else."

Ever since that talk, to this day I recall and heed his advice anytime I go for walks along pathways.

One Monday morning, as usual Dave came to work, along with the other clerks. He did not, however, go into the workroom, but headed towards the rear section of the general reading area. He sat at the table the entire day, mingling with the other library users. I ignored him, annoyed that this may be a new way of getting special attention. Next morning, when he came to work, he said that all weekend he had been high on drugs and he had too much respect for me to come into the library work area. I asked where he got the drugs. He laughed, saying it was available all over the prison. He said officers knew about this and some of them were involved.

I found it difficult to accept that the officers were engaged in drugs to the extent that prisoners described. My attitude changed when my part-time librarian shared her experience. This librarian had a full-time day job at a university library so her evening and weekend job in the prison were additional income. One Saturday morning she called to inform me that she was resigning from her job at The Pen. I asked why. She responded that she was tired of putting up with constant harassment from a certain senior correctional officer. Especially on weekends, the way he searched, frisked, and made comments about looking for contraband as she entered the prison, was humiliating. She said she felt she was being treated as if she was the criminal. Months after her resignation, I called her to inform her that the very same officer who harassed her constantly was fired because he was discovered bringing drugs into the prison.

David's Letter

5/10/92

Ms Shirley

Hi! Yes I heard that you left the Pen. I got a birthday card from Rm and she told me. You have been saying you were going to leave for the last two years. But I was surprise to hear from, but glad. I know you will like your new job. I think the challenge is more important to you than the money. Huh!!

I am working for S.U.I Metal shop #2 now as a clerk. We make tables, chairs, shelving, and most anything out of metal. It's not bad but the people are different. I had to cut my hair again to fit in the clan. There is more opportunity here if you are the right color. You know what I mean.

I seen Cal only two times when I first got here. I think he is in M.C.T.C. Now I'm sure. I had my first parole hearing last month. They told me to come back in five years (97). That's not too bad. They said when I come back up, I will get work release. I am going to end here. I wish you all the luck with your new job.

Take care

Dave. (Call me Dave I hate Howie, but use Howie on the addres

RJE

RJE was a fiftyish-year-old European American. He visited the library daily, reading reference books on electronics. He always asked me questions that I answered. His questions were never personal. He was always respectful. I was surprised to receive a beautifully scripted handwritten letter in the mail after he left The Pen.

20 November 1987
P.O. Box XXX
My dear Ms. Shirley

Although it is needless to say, By now you know that I was unable to return to the library goodbye to you. Please believe me when I write that, being unable to say goodbye to you, while being allowed the privilege of basking in the glow of your radiant beauty, one last time, was, and still is the only regret and a <u>very bitter regret</u> at that, which I have at my leaving the penitentiary this morning.

It is extremely rare to find a woman as intelligent as you working in a prison, and you have the physical beauty to match your intelligence. That is one of the rarest combinations of all. My fortune was in being able to meet you.

I was unable to say goodbye in person, so this letter is the next best thing(but for me a very poor substitute).

I think you would enjoy a brief description of my leaving. First my favorite lovely librarian informs me that I am departing. At that instant, I knew exactly what the words 'mixed emotions" mean. (I am certain that you know from what I have written above. After all for the last several months I have had the pleasure of trading jokes with you and gazing on the countenance of a very intelligent very beautiful woman—with **lust crazed eyes**—it really was a high point of my existence lately within the Penitentiary. For weeks I have pondered over the question of whether or not to inform you that you are currently starring in my fantasies. But I just did. Actually I had decided to walk up to you and look you in the eye and inform you that you had won my heart which made you eligible to try for the rest of me. I think that would have been a strong enough hint. Actually, now that I am far out of reach of your wrath, I feel secure in writing these words, truthfully, honestly, and sincerely.

After I got to my cell in the Pen, I was informed that my escort was waiting and I hurriedly packed. (Actually, threw would be a better word) my belongings in some boxes and I was processed in record time. Then placed in the transport van. I never got the opportunity to dash to the library like I wanted so much to do. You see, I gave my word to you and I particularly dislike breaking my word to you.

After being processed into the House of Corrections here in Jessup, I was placed in the cell I am in now, #48 segregation Unit. (That's one hell of a way to greet a visitor). But I am in this cell for temporary housing only).

You know after reading this letter and seeing all the mistakes I have in it, I am beginning to believe that this transfer has affected me more than I thought it did.

Well, I think I have used up all the time that you can afford to give to reading a letter from me.

I hope this letter gets to you without any problems. I also hope you do not catch any flak for receiving a letter from me.

I really would appreciate hearing from you So if you happen to have a minute or two, when you think of me in a non-profane way, that is, feel free to drop me a line. My address is: xx

Well, I really hate to do it, but I'M going to close. I hope to hear from you soon.

Sincerely, *RJE*

Sleep

Providing services to so many prisoners who arrive and depart according to their security levels, I don't always remember each individual. The writer below who calls himself "*Sleep*" is among those whom I cannot recall.

Sunday Evening 8/21/88
Hi Miss Shirley

I hope you are in good spirit and the library is running well. I saw Ms J, over here one day on my way to the Adjustment Hearing. They threw out the ticket. I asked her to say hello for me. Like I wrote Ro about a week ago explaining this jive. I would've wrote you sooner, but I hear you were on vacation. correct

I want you and Ro to know that this isn't my thing— and Mr. M. too. I knew nothing about it until the last minute and hardly believed them. You hear some many rumors in this place. Anyway, this administration just picked up a lot of old Timers figuring we knew what was happening and by not preventing it we incited it, ain't that something? The worst is yet to come—mismangement incited the incident and they still aren't addressing the problem. All they think of is punitive action. Not one of these kids give a damn about Supermax, just another new style jail, but still a jail.

Between you and I Shirley (if I may) these joints are failures anyway. They only make guys mean as hell. So back into the past goes Maryland as well. You have Warden R. who listen to anything they tell him, and then Actg. Chief of Sec. TH, who is a cross artist even among his peers, BS.

The only difference between him and us prisoners is we got caught. Then you have Major H. who is as crazy as a bed bug, and my favorite Major P. who's out of control and can't do his job, which incidentally he doesn't qualify for- lusting over the young boys in the population, he's queer as a three dollar bill. He got his rank by being in the right position at the right time, lucky for him, but his power is riding the backs of the "snitchers'. They really put him up there and that will be his downfall. Arhop, the Commissioner has the right idea, when you see a white man break from a position of authority, somethings up.

I predict that in the next Three to five years all hells going to break loose in this system, maybe sooner.

As of now I am still on Adm. Seg. Havn't been n lock-up for seven years. Haven't had a ticket in about five years. Doesn't make any difference with this admin.

We have some people working with and for us. I have some people working with me. Also I am trying to connect with the ACLU. I may just be the one to bust P's bubble. He should have left me to hell alone. Ro can tell you my charge is a deliberate lie. I was locked on Yard #1, and this guy has me running around with a baseball bat according to a "reliable source", yet I never hit anyone (smile) something else huh? They threw out the ticket yet here I am.

This isn't the type missive you write a state employee, but I feel it may come in handy to you some day. as you know knowledge is power. Plus, I consider you a very close friend. So take care of yourself. I hope to see you in a month or so, if things go well.

I have to respect you for your job and position. So I will just put it this way. I love you very much as a personal friend. (smile)

Sleep

PS. Sorry about thinking ahead of my pen its an old habit I should correct. This pen might truly prove mitier than the sword. It's the pen you gave me and believe me I have been working it.

Garth

Garth is a European American prisoner who visited the library frequently, always requesting Westerns and information on the Washington Redskins. He was pleasant, had great sense of humor, and always shared jokes with me. We knew he would be transferred to another institution, but not when. I was surprised to receive his letter that came through the post office.

Tuesday, May 16th '89

PO Boxxxx. Jessup

Dear Ms. Shirley,

Glenna, if I may, on this one and maybe only opportunity I hope of writing you. I just hope I spelled your first name properly. Please excuse my handwriting. I never did like English class anyway (smile)

Well, are you surprised to hear from me? Cause I'm certainly surprised that I'm writing you. I asked you in the library if I could write you and you said yes, but it would be your prerogative to write back. Well, only time will tell if you answer me.

Glenna, off the top I would like to say that I miss your lovely heart shaped face, your pretty eyes, your slender shape, and your subtle elegant beauty. A fine Jamaican lady you are. I hope to not embarrass you, but I speak from the heart. Many times I wanted to reveal my thoughts to you while I was there, but never could find the heart to because I am nothing more than a locked up convict without much hope for freedom anytime soon and I didn't want you to turn against me in dislike, so I kept my thoughts to myself and was content to say a hello and enjoy a periodic idle conversation with you. Even now I don't expect you to have any special feelings for me. I just wanted you to know that I really like you a lot, Glenna. I could reveal other thoughts I have of you, but then that would spoil my chance of hearing back from you. For if I told you everything, then your curiosity would quenched and you would thirst less to hear my words to tickle your ears and bring a smile to your face. I truly miss you Glenna. My sole purpose to go to the library daily as I did was to get a glimpse of eye contact with you. At times I felt something was there but I couldn't explore because of our total situation. I wanted you to have complete satisfaction in me that I wouldn't jeopardize your to lose your job.

I could get into more of what exactly I mean Glenna, but maybe right now you may feel I'm taking too much liberty with you as it is. If I've over stepped my boundaries, please except my apology. I don't mean to be crude, but there have been moments where I wanted to pull you up into my arms. Even address you by your first name on occasions, but bit my tongue in fear of uncertainty. You have to be very careful so as not to attract attention from the environment. Well Glenna, let me get on with the rest of this letter before I get too carried away. If I haven't already(smile) I'm sure you understand quite well where I stand. Now what is the mystery that is within you?

I've been down here now for 8 months and my status is still the same. Usually it is about a year process to find out whether or not you will be excepted, but with all of the turmoil that has been going on about this place I don't plan on knowing what my position will be for about another year. This place is miserable compared to the Penitentiary.

The only benefit this place offers is a possible early release. And you pay the price in more ways than one to get that release too. I imagine everything is the same old story up there with you at the library. Everyone trying to get a smile from you and at the same time trying to steal your books-:

You know Glenna, I would like to ask one favor of you, even if you don't write back. There is a library here, but only excepted prisoners are allowed its use. I know you get new World Almanacs every year. It is at all possible and if you have one on hand could you send me last years World Almanac. You know what a sports buff I am. I'd even be satisfied with an almanac that is 2 years old. It beats nothing. If that would be available you could mail it directly to me without any problem. Even used, I will get it.[9]

Also, if it's not too much trouble and it probably is (smile) could you send away for this court case for me through LASI. It is U.S. v Case 18 U.S.C. M.A. 535, 537. 40 C.M.R.247. I would really appreciate it if you would do that for me.

Glenna, I know you do not recognize the name of the return address on the envelope of this letter. I'm

---

[9] Direct mailing to prisoners is a rule violation. Information requests must go through the institutional librarian.

sure you remember me as Garth, but I don't know if you remember my last name is M...If you do then I may have a slimxxx of hearing back from you. Anyway, I don't want to put Garth M on the envelope for fear someone up there would recognize the name and maybe create a small problem for you. Everybody's business is nobody's business. Anyway the name on the envelope is an associate of mine or this tier, so if for some unknown reason this letter is returned it will find its way back to me.

I know it is kind of late to say this, but the Redskins stunk up the place last year, didn't they. I don't think they will do much this year either, but they may make the playoffs. Right now the basketball playoff are in full swing. I know you keep up with the basketball a little bit and that Michael Jordan of Chicago Bulls is really on a team? Isn't he. I really believe all year long that the Championship Finals was going to come down between the Detroit Pistons and Los Angeles Lakers, and I still believe it will happen like that. Los Angeles beat Detroit in 7 games last year and I believe with all my heart that Detroit will beat them this year in less than 6 games too. Well Ms. Shirley(smile) I hope I have not made a fool of myself. Which is a definite possibility, but regardless of what I do, I hope you enjoyed reading this letter and at least hearing from me, as much as I truly enjoyed writing to you. This letter is for no ones eyes, but yours.

Hopefully a friend. Garth
P.S. The M is for Matthew   I'm 38 – ALMOST

Donald E

March 21, 1990

Hello Ms Shirley

I pray this letter finds you in the best of health and still going strong. Thanks for the things you did for me while there, and even giving me some insight on a lot of things that I'll never forget. Tell Big O whatever he does do good on the computer, the little experience I did get on it I'll never forget. Tell Mrs. N. hello and may God bless her also. You both are beautiful people which I'll never forget in life.

I pray you were able to find someone to take care of the desk and be faithful at there work. Well I'm a clerk in the Dietary Dept. here. I also signed up for the Cooking and Baking program they have down here, it starts in October. The college program they have down here in Essex College is only two years. I plan to see how many credit they'll take. At least I can obtain an A.A. in counseling, or at least try. When I arrive at the institution, Ms B, the Librarian was out because of an accident she was involved in. The place just opened this week. But overall I like the job I'm doing. It's a blessing. This place is so clean plenty green grass and trees the air is fresh and the tension is low one reason so many are going home daily. Most of these guys only have two years or less. Well Ms Shirley you take care and continue to be a blessing for the men there even though I know some don't appreciate it, but I did.

A real friend

Donald E

Mark

Mark was good looking, lazy, talkative. He told some stories that I never knew whether to believe or ignore. He was very friendly. I fired him from the library job as he was too lazy and appeared to have been too close to one of the male corrections officers. This officer would walk up and call him away from his job, and in this environment, it is wise not to intervene since the officer could make life in the library a hell.

Mark's Letter

9/30/91

Monday Morning, 3:15am

'Hello Ms Shirley,'

Hoping this gift of thought has found you and family all doing well and life becoming more and more meanful for 'you' with each passing day.

As for myself, I'm fine regardless to the present situation. I am still in the southwing and living with the "Rumors" that very soon that all of us placed back here surrounding the C-Dorm incident will be transferring to the New Pen in Jessup. Regardless of how wrong or right such placement for those things accused.

So Instead of merely writing you with another form of request by itself, I decide to give you something "creative" to remember me by besides the "opinion" that I was "lazy" when I worked for you and of your clerks

I'll miss a lot about being here, some good friends, positive activities and goals not completed, but it's also said!

"That a wise man will make more opportunities than he finds, while a fool will die complaining about all he missed"..

So with that in mind, I truly look forward to the change, for surely it can't be any difficult than this New Administration here. I would like to ask three favors of you,

One, the address to ' The Chateau school of Cosmetology', here in Baltimore.

Two, Any recent copy of the City Paper (still trying to meet someone by way of the personals (smile)) and three,

I need three copies of 'something' that a friend or mine by the name of Jeff T will present to you in person due to the fact it 'may' get lost in the mail.

My tickets were dismissed without my having to appear, myself placed on admin seg without signing any advisement, nor have I seen a classification team since I've been back here (since 7/31), so I'm preparing 'legal suit'

'Thanks again for all', I'll miss you but you'll 'always' be unforgettable.

Take Care/Sincerely/Mark . P.S. Do give Mr. M. my regards

Leo

Leo was an English-speaking African-American prisoner who learned Spanish mostly from the books he requested on interlibrary loan. He knew I had a little knowledge of Spanish because there were two Spanish-speaking prisoners with whom I communicated. When I left The

Pen to work at the Howard County Public Library, Leon wrote me many letters in Spanish. The one below is an example.

A una amiga muy especial

Hola guapa

Ojala que al recibir esta cart ate encuentre bien y feliz.
Yo acabo de pensar que se me olvidara cuando recibi su mensaje. Me allegro que todo vaya bien contigo.
Yo estoy bien pero aburrido. La biblioteca no es la misma, sinti. Nada es la misma Pero bastante de eso.
No tenga verguenza dime todo!
Como estas verdaderamente? Como vaya su vida? Estas feliz? Como es tu trabajo Nuevo? Ganas much dinero, es facil o dificil? Y vas a colegio ahora?

Siempre Leo
Como se dice Be good

P.S Te extrano mucho Buena suerte. Espere que llegue a comprenderme.

Siempre Muchos carinos

My translation of Leo's letter:

Hello Good looking. I hope this letter finds you well and happy. I just began to think you forgot me when I receive your message. I am happy that all is well with you. I am fine but bored. The library is not the same without you

Nothing is the same, but enough of this. Don't be ashamed to tell me everything. How are your truly? How is your life going? Are you happy. How is your new job? Are you earning more money, is it easy or difficult? Are you going to college now.

Always Leo.
As they say: Be good.

PS I miss you a lot. Good Luck. I hope that you come to understand me.

Much affection

Hagerstown

Mi Persona Favorita

I trust and hope that this will find you well and in the highest of spirits.

As for myself? I'm fine, the best that can be expected considering the circumstances.

I haven't gone up for parole yet, but, even if I don't make it—I want to say to you; "thanks" with all my heart.

Your'e one of the kindest people I know, and somehow has restored my faith in the human race. In the midst of all the confusion, deceit and violence, youv'e been a guiding light and a welcome breath of fresh air. I don't say this lightly, but you will always have a friend in me.

Gracias por todo Para siempre. Leo

Hagerstown

Hola Senorita

Mucho tiempo sin verte, yo te extrano. Espero que todo este bien contigo. Me alegro mucho que tu has graduado. Dime, que clase de planes tu tienes ahora? Esta tu, felix con tu trabajo ahora, el dinero? (My Translation. Long time without seeing you. Hope that all is will with you. I'm happy that you have graduated. Tell me. Your plans now? Are you happy with your job now, the money?)

As for myself, I'm as well as can be expected. I'm continuing along the path of greater knowledge—there isn't a college program here, I've become a brick mason and also graduated a computer course that was given here (just a word perfect program). Perhaps in the future it'll come in handy. After all, knowledge is like money: the more you know, the more you will have:) I also go up for parole next month and this is why I'm using English. I was wondering would you write the parole board for me? You know just telling them something along the line of how long I'd worked for you, what my duties were, what learned & attitude etc.

I've included the address. And it you can't do it for some reason or another, I want you to know that it is perfectly understandable and that regardless I will always hold you in the highest of admiration.

This, you know is true, because you know enough about me to know that I've never lied to you. I've always been sincere.

Well I'm gone for now so until end for always;
Ten cuidado y portate.
Por Siempre
Leo

Kirk Bloodsworth

Child molesters were among the most hated groups in the prison system. They, like death row prisoners, were isolated from the general population. The institution allowed library services only by institutional mail or from a cart that visited the unit once per week.

Kirk Bloodsworth, sentenced to death for the sexual assault and death of a 9-year-old girl, was the first person in the United States to be exonerated using DNA sample. His story is documented in *Bloodsworth: The True Story of the First Death Row Prisoners Exonerated by DNA*, by Tim Junkin.

As the librarian, I never involve myself in any conversation about the nature of the crime of users, or express any personal sentiments regarding the individuals. I felt that my duty was to provide information to everyone in a nonjudgmental way. When Kirk sought information to prove his innocence, to me he was just another library user. In 1993, the news media were filled with stories about Kirk's innocence and his release from prison. In their various reports, the media stated that in the prison, Bloodsworth had read about DNA testing from a book, *The Blooding*, by Joseph Wambaugh. In this book, DNA testing helped solve two murders in Leicester, England. Bloodsworth requested a similar test through his defense attorney. It was the follow-up to this that ultimately proved his innocence.

After his release, I attended an event in Annapolis, where Kirk and his attorney were guest speakers. I reminded him that I was The Penitentiary Librarian when he was imprisoned. He hugged me.

"Miss Shirley, you saved my life. All those books helped me. When the prison administration didn't want to send any library cart, you had me be the person to take the books around the unit," he said.

From the podium, Kirk acknowledged my presence and thanked me again. At the end of the event his father came up to me.

"God bless you, young lady," he said.

In 2004, Kirk sent me the following email:

> To: gshirley@msde.state.md.us
> Subject: Prison Libraries
>
> Hi Miss Shirley
>
> It was so great seeing you again. . You helped me in so many ways. I thought how if I had'nt met you I may not of made it out as soon as I did. Thank you for everything.. KIRK BLOODSWORTH

FAREWELL

Towards the end of 1991, I knew it was time to leave The Pen because of my extreme discomfort with the new security chief. This short, foulmouthed pompous officer strutted around, shouted and spoke disrespectfully to everyone, especially the females. One day he marched into the library and started yelling at me in front of everyone. I turned my back, moved in the opposite direction, responding that I was not used to, nor expect to be spoken to, in that manner. I knew instinctively that this defiance, a challenge to his ego and authority, especially in front of the prisoners, placed me in a precarious position. His visits to the library became more frequent than any of his predecessors during my four years at The Pen. As he strutted around, it was obvious that he was looking for something, anything amiss to place restrictions on the library services or library staff.

The prisoners in general and my clerks in particular warned me to be careful of him because he had a reputation for collecting stories true or fabricated, by granting favors to snitches. They also said he used some prisoners to set up staff, and prisoners he did not like. These statements reminded me of the contents in a letter about him I received from a prisoner on lockup.

"Major X. who's out of control and can't do his job, which incidentally he doesn't qualify for—lusting over the young boys in the population, he's queer as a three dollar bill. He got his rank by being in the right position at the right time, lucky for him, but his power is riding the backs of the "snitchers'"

I noticed how the clerks and library users tensed up, and the atmosphere developed a stillness when he strutted in and around the library. For the first time in the prison environment, I felt uncomfortable, not with the prisoners, but a senior member of the security staff. I knew that because of my defiance, he was waiting and looking for an opportunity to "set me up." It was time to leave.

December 1991, I negotiated and accepted a job offer from Howard County Public Library. The system had received funding under the Library Service Construction Act (LSCA)[10] to set up a library at the county's detention center. The library administrator offered to hire me at the minimum salary level of the Master's degree with the provision that I obtain the American-accredited Master's in Library Science degree within a specified time. The salary offer was much less than what I was earning at The Pen, but the move would give me some flexibility at this juncture in my professional career to get the American-accredited library degree. I negotiated working two evening shifts in the public library and three day shifts setting up and eventually operating library services at the detention center. The evening shift enabled me to attend morning classes at the University of Maryland, where in 1993 I graduated with a Master of Library Science degree.

The week before I left The Pen I received an outpouring of sentiments, verbally and through letters and cards from the prisoners. My last workday, the library clerks as usual were the last to leave the building. Dressed in heavy winter coats, they stood in line waiting for the corrections officer's permission to exit the building.

As the officer shouted, "Count time," I stood by the entrance area in plain sight of the officer and as each clerk approached me with outstretched hands for a goodbye, I declared loudly enough for everyone to hear, "Now that I can't get in trouble I can give each of you a goodbye hug. But don't any of you try to get fresh."

Completely unexpected, the hugs from each were brief. As Dondee hugged me,

with deep regret in his voice he said, "Ah, gee, if I knew you were going to do that, I would not have put on my heavy coat so soon. That way I could really feel the hug."

"Take what you get and quit complaining," I retorted with a laugh.

---

[10] In 1995, name changed to Library Service Technology Act (LSTA).

Farewell Letter from Dondee:

TRUE THOUGHTS

My heart skip beating—for that big
moment I was froze, to hear that you
are leaving really stiffened my toes!
We had a lot of fun, we have
Shared a lot of laughs, we have to me
Shared precious thoughts that will
Last and last and last!
I surely hope this not over or just
Another something in the past, because
I really do enjoy you and hope you will not dash.
You have given me good advice,
Friendly guidance that was always
Right, you have kept me thinking and
Pondering into the late hours of the night.
I know once you are gone things wont
seem too bright, I am going to miss
you physically—but mentally we will still be tight.
Well. I guest I must confess you
Really are the best: you are smart,
Tricky, and cunning—you won't fall
for anything less!
I am so sorry I did not get to hold you
or to squezz you really tight
but I realize in our positions it may
not be to bright.
I'm really going to miss you, for

you are the best I never had, but one
thing I can truthfully say: you really
make a good and to have known you
really makes me glad.
So, please take care of yourself
Wherever you go and keep me
In your memories and perhaps we two will
Grow!

Christmas Card

To Shirley From Dondee

May God Bless and keep you in His
Unchanging Hands.
Wishing you the best where eer you go
And whatever you do, It's been a
Pleasure working with you.
Wishing you many Christmas's to come
Even though you choose to run.
I will miss you and I always did care
That's why Im also wishing you a
Happy New Year.
Take this card with you where ever you
Go, so that you will always remember
The Big "D"

Merry Christmas and a Happy New Year

++Dear Ms Lady

Working with you has been an educational experience and may I say a joy. It has also been a pleasure
working with a real lady. Not that I want you to go—
but it's not up to me you see.

Where ever you go, I want you to remember M and
remember E- put them together and remember me.

The Big "D" is always a good person to know.

Love is what makes the world go around, because
God is Love and he made the world. What so good
about good by because all it does is makes you cry.

February 12, 1992

Ms. G. Shirley
Howard County Library
Dear Ms. Shirley,

Well, hello!...there stranger and how might you be
doing these days?

Hopefully, everything is working-out for the best
in your corner. I was and still am delighted to hear from
you, at least we know that you have not forgotten us
just yet.

Well, I guest I must tell you this: Things are not
going to well for me in the business area. Why? Because this lady here gives me a real bad hard time, I
think she really hates me or at least wants to kill me
for some unthinkable reason. Nevertheless, I'm still

hanging in there trying to get the job done one day at a time.

(I)– We really miss you! Why not come in one day and take a look around and see if it is the same as you left it. Hopefully, they do not close it down, because if they do; I will not have anywhere to work. That spells (N O M O N E Y).How awful to consider the mistake of not making ANY MONEY AT ALL! I would probably go even crazyier that I already am.

However, I appreciate your unselfish thoughtfulness and hope that you will enjoy Valentine's Time Day as much as you would like to. Don't be disturbed because The "Cool" Don didn't send you a card. You know me, I do not hardly believe in these so-called holidays these people come up with. But I guess I will anyway

VALENTINE'S DAY GREETING

Greetings and salutations to a strength and courage, to a fighter and none quitter, to a person of big heart.

Keep believing in yourself—your ability to think. Change Things for the future so unselfish care, love, friendship And determination will not die!

May you find your desired dream and conquer any fear, Anything that may hinder your forward motion.

DonDee

Burk-Bey

Burk-Bey, like many prisoners, converted to Islam in prison. He constantly questioned me about Jamaica, and other social issues, saying he had not had previous discussions with intelligent black women.

A Kwanzaa Card Kujichagulia from Burk-Bey

Dear Ms Shirley

This card is to thank you for everything and to let you know that you will be MISSED around here. ALSO, I wish you the best in the future.

Very Truly Yours
Burk-Bey

Christmas Card...

Mrs Shirley

Just a note to say Merry Christmas and A Happy New Year

As I understand you are leaving me taking away Some of the sunshine and beauty from my life.

I understand it's not personal so with that in mind, I wish you will in your future pursuits. You will be sorely missed.

If you pass this way again, be sure to smile on me, otherwise

I'll see you in Jamaica.
Warm regards.
Mendy

Post-Penitentiary Cards and Letters ++KV

12/12/92
Glendon,

I hope I spelled your first name right (probably not)
But Miss Shirley sounded impersonal since I'm going to be a civilian (haha) soon. How is everything going, I hope my replacement is doing good. I know I left it kind of a mess (halfway organized). My spelling is probably terrible. Your lucky if you even get to the library but the place is in a much more organized way with total respect for the C.O. If you have the time to write, could you give me your address and best hours to visit you at the library in Columbia. If not I get out on or about the 20th of January. I know my handwriting gotten pretty sloppy from lack of use. I'll probably visit you sometime in January, unless you happen to know any nice unattached women between 21 and 31 that would go out with an ex-prisoner. You taught me a lot about having faith and trust in people especially women for which I'll always be grateful. I'm getting so excited about getting out soon that am counting hours now. I

hope you have a nice Christmas and safe new year.

Sincerely
KV
PS. I still got my order form for the chameleon

RQ

December 8, 1993. 2pm
Mrs. Shirley

Hope your Holiday has been the best that you wanted and received the things you hoped for. I'll be doing back to court to have my sentence reduced in Jan- next month and hope the outcome will be in my favor. I never said to you anything about my charge; the real thing is I shouldn't be here. I eyewitness my codefendant and another guy beating this guy up & I helped the guy up to see if he was all right. When he got to the hospital the police asked him who was there, he really didn't see anyone but he knew I was there by talking to him and my co-defendant by voice. The third he said he didn't know. He knew all three of us because he drinks with us. I don't blame him. I blame my co-defendant. The guy only told what he heard and assumed. So the police charge me and him cause we was the only names he could come up with.

David my co-d was locked up before I was and instead of him telling then they were charging the wrong person he shoved the weight.

I asked him why he didn't tell them, his only reply was he couldn't remember the last name, so he told them "we" just wiped him. By him saying we, he tied me into a crime I didn't do.

The lawyer said the state wasn't going to spend the money finding the third person cause the victim named us and he said we gave them a shut case. So I'm here and Will's where I should be on the outside. If I had tried the case it was a very big chance I would be found guilty, so I had to take an Alfa Plea for nothing.

And that's how I got in this mess. It don't pay at times to help someone and I don't have realy any thing to say to me co-defendant because he knows I'm wrongfully here. That's' that for now.

I asked to write you because it would give me some one on the outside to explain what's going on here and how I feel. Its very hard to do here and not the right place. The majority of people here has no value on human life or things around them. To socialize and get along is a lost cause when they don't care.

I do talk to some of the people /all of them not bad. I makes a difference to know that some one will write or thinking of you, then the time doesn't bother you as much as to know your just here and that's it. I left a card to be given to you. I hope you understand the meaning of it and liked it. MY D.O.C. number is xxxx510

You have to put it on the letter in order for me to get it I haven't seen Classification yet, when I do I'll know what institution I'll be in. I'm trying for min security if I can. I also put in yesterday to see when I be coming up for parole hearing.

I have 225 days in on the time they will take off here, so it will get me closer. I can see out around the city a little. I'm on the fourth floor. Things are moving a little slow at the time when it pick up and I know were I'll definitely be I'll write again. Hope this doesn't bother you or make a problem be waiting to hear from you. Best wishes for the Holidays

RQ

An undated handwritten note from Richie inspired me to use his words, *Here in This Place of Monotony and Despair,[11]* as the title of a chapter I wrote in the book *Advances in Librarianship*, edited by the University of Maryland iSchool professors.

---

[11] *In a Place of Monotony and Despair: A Library!* Glennor Shirley. Advances in Librarianship. Vol. 42. *Celebrating the James Partridge Award: Essays toward the Development of a More Diverse, Inclusive, and Equitable Field of Library and Information Science,* by Diane L. Barlow and Paul T. Jaeger.

Chapter 6
Howard County Detention Center, January 1992

The state government administration is responsible for prisons while county administration run detention centers and jails. Detention centers house individuals who are awaiting trial or sentenced for less than two years. My experiences working at The Pen did not prepare me for Howard County Detention Center (HCDC) but educated me on the major differences between prisons and detention centers. I also saw the racial inequities that lead to higher incarceration and longer sentencing of nonwhite individuals.

The population of approximately 200 detainees, including approximately ten females, had a higher level of education than the average Penitentiary prisoners. Most of these detainees were white, had reading interests, information needs, and behaviors that were very different from the men in The Penitentiary. Puzzled by the racial differences, some detainees enlightened me. They said drug dealers primarily from Baltimore City and Prince Georges County travelled to Howard County to sell dope to the rich white people who were mostly young guys.

"Because they would stand out too much if the white people come to us in the hood," one detainee said. They also said that family members of white detainees often claimed that the offender had mental health issues, emphasizing that they would seek therapeutic and psychological help to treat the problems of their incarcerated family member. The outcome was reduced or no sentencing for many or the white offenders.

The Detention Center library area was under construction. A small room became the temporary library, providing information mainly through request forms I placed in housing units. To ensure the relevant information for users, I conducted surveys with the incarcerated men and women and visited other detention centers throughout the state. I communicated with the warden, chiefs of security, classification managers, corrections officers, and the outreach administrator in the public county library, seeking insights on protocols, budget, and collection development. Collections included books and audiovisual materials on business plans, job interviews, resumes, self-esteem, family relations, resources for drug treatment centers, and leisure reading books from *The New York Times* Bestseller List.

At The Pen, African-American library users had very little interest in science-fiction books. At the detention center, users constantly requested this genre. The number of Spanish-speaking detainees increased so I added materials on English as a second language. This language collection was helpful to the men since several of them were illiterate in their first language. My interaction with the center's GED instructors also provided insight on procuring materials to meet the needs of the low-level readers.

Detention Center Journal

2/5/92

Tammy is back, looking subdued. Day one she does not look at me. I ask her, "What about all those promises you made about not coming back to a place like this?" She looks sheepish, smile, and makes some inarticulate sounds, remaining quiet.

2/14/92

Today, two things make me think of the men with whom I worked at The Pen. First is that the Detention Center library clerk, Mary, is a woman. I am not used to working with female prisoners. Second, I receive a beautiful Valentine card from Dondee, the penitentiary prisoner who on my last day at The Pen said I should have pre warned them that I would give a farewell hug, before he put on his heavy coat.

Conversation with Mary

Mary is one of the older detainees. She works in the library, dusting and cleaning the shelves. At first, she was reserved. A few days after working with me in the library, she has become more relaxed, and vocal.

"The jail in Montgomery County is real nice."

"You have been to that jail too, and in Jessup, and you have a detainer in Virginia! You make this a habit!" I laugh.

"Well, a person got to eat and pay bills and the crowd I mixed with were into the same thing, so it kinda follow naturally." She flicks the duster on the books, pauses, and looks at me.

"What did you do, breaking and entering or robbery?" I ask.

She shakes her head emphatically.

"No. Clothes. I don't rob nobody or interfere with they things. I'm into clothes."

"Where did you get them?"

She looks at me as if to say, "Where do you think?"

"Stores," she replies.

"How did you do it without being caught?" I look up from my files, because while I am talking to her, I have been writing and placing headings for vertical files.

"Just walked out with them in big bags." She purses her lips contemplatively as if deciding how much to say to me. "Look, I see them white women with them big packages walking out the store and nobody stop them, so I just did the same thing. I even walk out with a mink coat once from L and X."

"What did you do with the clothes you take?"

"Sell them or keep some of them for myself. I into clothes and I like nice things, so if I like something, I keep it." She warms to the topic, speaking more freely. "Well, it kinda hard to get rid of them sometimes so I got me a fence and we make a deal and I get a percentage."

"But the clothes have security systems."

"I know how to remove them and sometimes I keeps a clipper with me, so ah can get them off."

"How were you caught?"

She looks sheepish. "When you high you tend to do foolish things and that day, I was high." She approaches me with a kind of conspiratorial air, stops by the desk and places her hands on her chin. In a contemplative manner she continues.

"That is why ah don't like to go stay at my daughter's. All the problems, bills, everything. I just started up the drugs again."

"You did drugs, what did you take?"

"Cocaine, heroin, but I haven't done any for a long time now. I don't want to go back to my daughter's when I leave this jail."

She moves towards the cart and begins to vigorously wipe the black cart that held some books. A few minutes later she turns towards me.

"I tried to keep straight, but with my husband in prison, and me alone with four children, I had to find a way."

"Tell me, Mary," I say, halting my work for a moment in order to face her. "Your husband, son, and you are in jail. Is that what happens to most of the people with whom you relate or associate?"

"Hmm-hmm." She looks at me, leans over the counter with one hand pressed against her cheek. "You see all your friends doing the same thing, and sometimes we all in jail together, it is difficult to keep out of trouble, and the bills have to pay. But this time I'm serious, I'm not going to jail again after I leave here." She moves once more toward the cart and begins dusting. "It's too noisy in the cells. I can't get a moment's peace, and sometimes I like it quiet." She looks at me, puts the sponge on the cart, stands midway between the cart and the area where I am sitting.

"You wouldn't think that, the way I been talking since I came in here."

"It's okay," I say. "I seem to have that effect on people."

Feb. 26, 1992

Steph

Steph, my new detention center clerk, is a short 30-year-old woman who looks much younger, weighs about 120 lbs., and claims she has gained about 15 pounds since she is in jail. She has light brown skin tones, large eyes that peer out from under long black lashes. The front of her hair is cut short. The rest is braided. The baritone voice coming from such a small person is surprising. I constantly remind her to tone down.

"Today is 83 days and I have 50 more days to go. I been counting every day. I ain't going to no jail again."

She shakes her head. I see eyes full with determination and pain.

"No," she says. "I can't understand how these guys go in and out of jail. I ain't ever going to jail again."

"What brought you to jail in the first place?" Asking the females questions comes more easily that when I was in the male prison. If you ask the male prisoners, some of the men may easily interpret it as personal interest, and that often leads them to fantasizing about future relationships. Here in this jail, the women willingly volunteer the information.

"Check," she says in a matter-of-fact tone. "I was working in this office and I took some checks. Three years ago too."

She tilts her head backwards and laughs.

"I did the check good. No one could tell I forged the signature." She laughs again. "I lucky that I only get six months because the amount could have been a felony charge. My lawyer was good."

She shifts in the chair, looks at the officer across the room, and continues to talk.

"I didn't check with my parole officer. Didn't even know who she was. Police couldn't find me." She lets out a sort of groan and then laughs again.

"Is my mother let them catch me. I was visiting her and the police come to the house, and ask for me by name." Again she tosses back her head and laughs. "I say to the police, 'She ain't here, no one by that name here.'" She continues laughing, then says, "My mother shouted out from inside, 'Stop that now, and give yourself up, and get over with it.' That's how they caught me."

She spreads her fingers, looks at her hands, and says, "Three years!" She looks around the little area that is the library. "No way. I ain't coming back to this place again."

6/4/92. JT

JT has tattoos all over his arms. He says each one represented some philosophy, theology, or some girl he either dated, or with whom he was in love. His various occupations included doing tattoos for $100 per hour for customers who were doctors, lawyers, and other professional people.

"You just don't see it because sometimes it's a small symbol and it's hidden. Many people with tattoos wear long sleeves. The heat from the sun will drain the dye, so it's better to cover them," he said.

JT, an avid science-fiction reader, says that most books in the library collection are rereads for him. Today he will not borrow many books because he feels he will be leaving the jail soon. I think he is leaving the prison system, but he says no, he would be leaving for a state prison, and a long sentence. He had already spent 15 years in the prison system.

"You must like it, since you commit another offense to return."

"No," he replies. "The prison system does not prepare you to go back into society. You spend the greater part of your life in prison. There, everything is done for you. People tell you what to do every step of the way. You don't have to worry about rent or any other form of expense. Then you are placed back in society. You are confronted with the pressures, people's behavior, expenses, and so many negative forces. You were never taught or prepared to cope with these. It is very easy to find the easiest way out."

"You articulate the problems very well, so having identified them, I expect you would have been one of those who could cope."

He laughs. "The judge said the same thing, but you have to understand it is one thing articulating, it is another thing to actually deal with it."

He would have continued, but it is time for him to leave. He had chosen to spend his allocated recreation time in the library talking to me. Now he must return to his cell.

2/5/93

Each day I learn something new in the correctional environment. Today, shortly after Lisa enters the library, she tells me how she makes grilled cheese in her cell.

Lisa's detention center cooking successes:

Grilled Cheese

Take the cheese and put it between the bread.

Place it on a piece of paper.

Heat the iron and keep it on till the cheese melts.

Turn over, and do the same on the other side.

Voila—grilled cheese!

Hot Coffee

Put the liquid in the soda can

Place it on the iron—easy

Or, get wires and place in liquid. It works.

Lisa continues.

"This time is much better than when I was here last year. They wouldn't pay me much, though I work hard, very hard. So I just took me one of those."

Her chin tilts towards my computer. She is about 5'4", light brown complexion, shaved head, doe-like eyes, full lips, dressed in sweat-suit with green, white and red patterns. Detention center rumor is that Lisa had a bottle of cologne, and at her disciplinary hearing she told the officer he could take it since it is contraband in the prison.

"If you use it," she told the officer, "you can't keep the women off you." Lisa is gay.

Potty

He hops into the library, bouncing from one shelf to the other. His dirty-looking crushed T-shirt makes me think that at one time it was white. His tufted, bushy hair looks as if it has not been in contact with a comb or any barber's instrument for months. He says he is wearing dreadlocks.

He skips from shelf to shelf, ending up at the information desk with three science-fiction titles. I am surprised at the choice of books, wondering if he is mentally unstable. He signs his name on the borrower's card, fidgeting from one foot to the other, rocking his head as he bops out of the library. Next visit he selects more science-fiction titles and talks with a few of the other prisoners about titles he had read. Could he read the books at such a rapid rate? I wonder. He asks me for some titles that are not in our collection. I hand him a request form. The third time he hops into the library, his hair is cut very short.

"Your hair looks nice, what happened?" I ask.

"Oh, they gave me a haircut. They brought me in here before I could do anything about my hair." He laughs.

I hand him the books he had requested. He requests more.

"I've read everything in this series," he says. "I love fantasy and science-fiction. Everyone I associate with think I am crazy to read these, but I like to go off into that world. Look what reality brought me!" He sweeps his hands around, his body following his hands in the swoop. That day is the beginning of many conversations between Potty and me whenever he visits the library. I am the initiator of some of the conversations because I realize he is very intelligent.

"I spend a lot of time on drugs. One thing a drug dealer learns to do is keep time," he tells me.

His hands join the sweeping motion of his head as he laughs, hopping up and down.

"If you don't keep time the competition is around the corner, ready to cut in on you." His hands that never stop their sweeping gestures swoop down. "I would take an hour to do my transactions and the rest of the day is mine."

One day Potty spent the entire time in the library telling me all about drugs. He described the effects, the mixtures, the cultivating, and manufacturing conditions. The corrections officer on duty and I listened to detailed accounts of the lightning, soil, and seasonal conditions for the cultivation of marijuana. To my unschooled mind this unabashed detailed description was amusing and fascinating. Potty's knowledge of the conditions of cultivating marijuana was so extensive that the correctional officer asked him what kind of lighting would be appropriate for his home flower garden. Potty gave information on the type of lighting, the manufacturer, and the cost.

"With such an extensive knowledge, you should be in horticulture," the officer said.

"I was. And man, I produced the best marijuana. I'll be out of this jail soon. But when I leave, I owe a man $16,000 for some dope. This is what they caught me with," Potty said as he threw back his head and laughed.

"Won't he understand that you were in jail?" I asked.

"That is not his concern, he gave me the goods, and it was my stupidity why I got caught. It is unfortunate, but as I leave jail, I will have to make some money to pay him back or I will be in trouble."

He bounced in a few days later, head shaved. He chose some books, then said, "Great news, I have ten more days in here."

"Great," I said. "I don't want to see you after that."

He laughed, talked about how he was going to get high and called out the name of the substance he would be using.

"It gives you a great feeling," he said. "I was once in a drug program but they drove me out because I said I was not a drug addict."

The officer laughed, saying he was an addict. Potty emphatically denied this. He named the drugs he took and said he could do without them anytime he wished. He told us that he stayed away from them whenever he felt he was not acting right. To this the officer stated that he never acted right anyway, and with the drugs he was in no condition to decide. Potty informed the officer that he studied the drugs and knew that some, like marijuana, were not addictive.

His story about his $16,000 debt was an eye-opening fact about corrupt police officers.

"You know the police always suspicious of some cars with New York and Florida licenses on Route 95, because they figure it is drugs. I hitched a ride with some guys and the car had a New York license plate and they stop us. When they searched the trunk and lift up the spare tire they find drugs and $20,000 in cash. I really didn't know they had so much. The police arrested us and charge us with possession of drugs and $10,000 in cash. That means they keep ten thousand dollars for themselves. When I get out I have to pay my debt. The drug dealer is not concerned with my problems."

"Didn't you tell the judge that you had more cash with you and the officers didn't declare it?"

"You crazy, miss, then the judge would give us longer sentences."

4/28/1993

Sandy is back in the detention center. As she enters the library, she and some other detainees look at a photograph I had taken of her and another woman in the library. She tells them that Mary was the other female beside her in the photo, but Mary was dead. They continue their conversation as if they were discussing the weather. A few days after Sandy's announcement about Mary's death, the interlibrary loan package I received included the book on menopause that Mary had asked me to get for her. She had shared with me her many physical discomfort at this stage in her life. I had promised to get information for her but she left the institution before the material arrived.

Joseph

He enters the library. One of the quiet patrons. Neatly dressed, long sleeves, fine striped shirt, brown trousers. His white hair is brushed back, in a somewhat unruly fashion. Because of his looks, the detainees call him Einstein.

His stay in the detention center is brief. When it was time for him to leave the center for time served, he refused to leave. The officers placed handcuffs on him, then escorted him out. The prisoners laughed as they told me that Joseph swore he would go to a supermarket and steal a piece of meat so he could be rearrested.

I remember Joseph from my job on the information desk at the County Library. He was very quiet, computer savvy, and always carried two very large garbage bags. Approximately half an hour before the library closed, he would go and conduct his daily ablutions in the men's restroom. At the onset of winter he deliberately committed minor offenses, like throwing a chair at a patron, aware the police would be called and he would go to jail. Some said he was a veteran but refused to stay in the confines of homeless shelters. After I retired and visited the public library as a user, I would see Joseph sitting almost always at the same computer area, just like he did 20 years previously. For me this was a great testament of the importance of libraries as a temporary refuge and a mentally safe haven for many homeless persons.

Lashonda

Slim, tall, brown skin, wide full lips, wide, sleepy-looking eyes, black shoulder-length hair, straightened and combed in a different style each day. Looking at her gives one the impression of someone frail, delicate, with a soft voice. When she first visited the library, she read only romance novels. I suggested other authors. She liked them. As she became comfortable with me, she asked about black history books. I gave her Marcus Garvey, *Before the Mayflower*. After that, her appetite for similar books became insatiable. Sometimes we discussed the evolution of black people—not with much depth as neither of us had the knowledge. She shifted to reading a lot of black history information and began recommending titles to her cellmates. She was obviously an influence because the women would come into the library and say, "Lashonda say I must get...."

One morning, a user came into the library and picked up a book on witchcraft and magic.

"Please, please, I beg you...," Lashonda said,

Her passionate plea resulted in the woman smiling sheepishly as she said, "Okay," returning the book to the shelf.

Lashonda handed her *The Autobiography of Malcolm X* as she said, "Here, read this."

10/5/93

HW walks in the library. His eyes look tired, his face drawn.

"I'm on work release," he says. "But guess where they have me?"

"Where?" I and some of the library clerks ask him as he leans against the information desk.

"In a bar, sweeping. Me—with a DUI and assault charge—an AA candidate."

"Oh, Lord, oh, no," we exclaim.

The corrections officer burst out laughing.

"I can handle it, though," he says. "If I find it getting too much, I'll quit."

He stretches his hand towards me.

"I thank you for all you did to get me out this place. I was able to escape mentally with all these books you lent me. I really appreciate it."

He had lost weight, his eyes look glazed, as if he is ill. He has his shirt on the wrong side.

"Good luck," I say as he walks out the library door.

Eric

Eric's mother and I attended events outside the prison. I was surprised when she confided that her son was at the detention center and she was the one who called the police as his alcoholism had gotten out of control. He was very intelligent and had traveled overseas to many countries with his mom and dad. Although he was young, abuse of alcohol gave him many wrinkles. His blond hair and beard looked straggly with hints of gray. I gave him a job in the library. After he left the prison, I received a letter from him.

Dear Ms Shirley

I want to thank you for the opportunity and pleasure of working with you in the library.

It was the only bright spot in my stay here. I wish you the best and hope to see you again under other circumstances. Peace.

Eric

Musings

July 22, 1995

It is now five weeks since I left the detention center library for a promotion to work full time in the public library. What a change! "Assistant branch manager" sounds more prestigious than "detention center librarian." Everyone says that I must be happy to be where I am now, away from the prison environment. I mused briefly on some aspects of my experiences in public and prison libraries. To me the challenges of working in prison libraries may be different, but no greater than working in a public library.

The detention center, like the penitentiary prisoners, housed non-traditional library users. Majority of these individuals said that the prison library was the one positive place in their negative punitive setting. They expressed appreciation that in spite of their crime, I was nonjudgmental and provided them with their information needs in an impartial way. I received a lot of respect. The three years I worked at the detention center, there was only one individual who initially behaved disrespectfully. This white male shouted at me, demanding what he wanted in a very pompous manner. Each visit, whenever he yelled, I responded in a very calm voice, asking him to repeat his request since I neither listen nor respond to people when they shouted like he was doing. By his fourth visit, he realized that I was unresponsive to his rude behavior and toned down communicating in a more civil manner. The result was that he got the information he requested, and my reaction sent a message to other library onlookers.

Like penitentiary prisoners, detention center library users encouraged the recently incarcerated to visit the library, explaining that the librarian would help. Initially, many new detainees came acting hostile or frightened, not expecting to get any positive responses. In a defiant manner, a few of them would ask for items they thought were bizarre and unsettling. Others asked for books on exorcism, witchcraft, or how to be a serial killer. One prisoner claimed that he wanted to be the first black serial killer in the United States. Instead of joining the laughter of the others who were listening, my response was to conduct a reference interview. "Are you interested in the history of the topic, the actual crime, legal aspects," etc. Many of them were surprised and pleased that I took the time to get the information, even if they initially meant it to be hilarious so they could enjoy my discomfort. Soon their requests became more traditional and they gradually moved from the stage of wonder, to criticizing the library about unavailable items. I considered the criticism a success. It meant that they were expecting from their prison library the same services as those users outside the walls.

In contrast to the detention center, many of the public library patrons with whom I had daily contact were predominantly middle-class individuals of all ages, gender, and race. The county ranks as the richest county in Maryland and the third-highest median-household income in the nation[12]. The branch where I worked was in an area with many African-Americans, and was one of the county's two lower-income neighborhoods. Mornings, the librarians were busy dealing with stay-at-home mothers and toddlers attending story hours. It was also the meeting place for homeschoolers and their children. These groups, predominantly white, were often very demanding. I recall one visitor shouting at librarians to justify demands, "My tax pay your salary." Located next to the elementary and middle schools, and near to the high school, each afternoon the library became host to many unattended afterschool children. They ran around in the library, shouted, cursed, deliberately flooded the toilets, and once placed a fart bomb between books on the shelves. They used profanities to the librarians when asked to modify their behaviors, or to leave the library. Once my response to the complaint of an irate parent was:

"Please do not tell me it is racism because the librarian asked your child to leave the library when he told her to 'fuck off,' calling her a 'Ho' when she asked him to stop running and shouting in the library."

I had heard the children saying "Ho" many times to staff, and thought it was just a meaningless American expression until one staff member realized I was clueless and educated me.

"In the hood, Glennor, it means 'whore.'"

Before the availability of computers in many households, on the eve of their child's assignment, some parents strode in the library a few minutes before closing and expressed annoyance that all materials on

---

[12] Yeager, Amanda. "Howard ranks second in nation in median income...." *Baltimore Sun,* November 16, 2015. http://www.baltimoresun.com/news/maryland/howard/ellicott-city/ph-ho-cf-howard-income-1003-20130930-story.htm.

the topic were already checked out, demanding to know why at fifteen minutes before closure the library was announcing that the photo-copiers and printers would be turned off. They could not get to the library before because they were involved in their children's soccer games, band practice, or similar activities.

I assigned nomenclature to three of my regular public library users: Mr. Erotica, Mr. Butt Lover, and Mr. Flasher. Mr. Erotica spent about three to four hours on the computer. Staff received constant complaints from parents who saw and said they did not want their children exposed to the pornography he was viewing. When I spoke to him about his viewing pornography, he informed me of his Constitutional rights.

Mr. Butt Lover wore wide-legged, very short shorts. He would crouch on the ground as if examining materials on the lowest shelf in various sections of the library. Meanwhile, the big-butt woman near him is bending, examining books, completely unaware that his nose was so close to her rear end. One backward move would have resulted in collision between nose and buttocks. Whenever Butt Lover saw me approaching, his head would quickly bend down to the shelf as if examining the contents, so it was difficult to confront him. When I asked the male library staff to keep an eye on this patron because of his behavior, another staff member laughed and said, "You mean the guy in the short-short red shorts? I was wondering why he pull his shorts up so high."

Mr. Flasher darted among the shelves, exposing himself to the school-girls, then rushed out the library by the time they came to alert staff. He would stay away for some time, so it was difficult to identify him.

I loved working in the public library. Like the prison library, it was the safe and nonjudgmental place to provide information, relevant pro-grams, technology, and collections to meet the information needs of all users. I just did not consider working in the public library environment any less challenging than working in a prison library.

One day I spent 20 minutes talking to noisy and rambunctious afterschool children. I told them I did not want to call the police because when I worked as a prison librarian, majority of the library users were persons of color. They were intrigued, asked many questions. One girl said her brother was in the juvenile system and it was very tough on her mother. That day they were quiet and well behaved.

Chapter 7

Back in Prison!

After earning a Master's degree in Administration from Johns Hopkins University, and a Master's in Library Sciences from University of Maryland, I became branch manager in Howard and Baltimore counties' libraries, before going back in the prison environment, echoing the words of some prisoners.

"The money was good." Money, however, was not the sole lure. I recalled how as prison librarian at The Pen and Howard County Detention Center, the position enabled me to make positive differences in the lives of prisoners. I remembered the comment from a prisoner when he came to bid me farewell on my last day at the detention center. He said to the public defender, "If you ask me, they should ask Ms. Shirley to go to all the prisons to teach them about rehabilitation. I'm 59 years old, I dropped out of school and had no interest in finishing, now for the first time she has me thinking about getting GED."[13]

This new position as Library Coordinator, with overall responsibility for the state prisons' libraries, would enable me to exercise greater influence on prison libraries, their users, and to initiate community partnerships and collaborations, especially on reentry issues. I had the prerogative to visit all the Maryland prison libraries, engage in dia-

---

[13] "Paroled! A Librarian Leaves Jail." https://olos.ala.org/columns/?p=107.

logues, and get input from prisoners, librarians, and prison administration at the various locations across the state.

My second entry into the prison system was very similar to when I accepted the job at the Maryland Penitentiary. The position had been vacant for about six months and there was no one to educate me on rules pertaining to administrative protocols, budget, relations with the various libraries, librarians, and principals across the state. While challenging, I saw it as an opportunity to stamp my own footprint. I perused files, initiated discussions, and visited the prisons librarians across the state seeking feedback that would enable more relevant and effective administrative support. I joined the American Library Association (ALA), Association for Specialized and Cooperative Library Agencies, Prison Library group, (ASCLA)[14] a section of ALA, with a dynamic and dedicated number of prison librarians across the country. They shared information on budgets, programs, providing services, and their individual state's interpretation of "Access to the Courts."

At the coordinating level, it did not take me long to become aware of the differences among prison administrators, librarians, and the libraries they supervised. Majority of the librarians were proactive and cooperative, working with me as I initiated and developed programs that included Family Literacy, book discussions, displays, purchasing relevant materials that met not only the popular reading interests of prisoners, but materials that would assist in reentry. At the other end of the spectrum, the performance of a small number of librarians made me think of them as "Prison Librarians doing time." They go to work, guard the books, leave work on time, often using institutional restrictions as justification for their stasis. During a visit to one of the libraries, for example, I observed a librarian acting like the security guard for the

---

[14] ASCLA Organization. http://www.ala.org/ascla/asclaourassoc/aboutascla.

books. This individual kept popular reading materials behind the glass window in the work room. Whenever library users desired a book, the librarian and potential borrower conducted a series of finger and facial communication as if they were both deaf. From behind the glass cage, the librarian pointed to the books on the shelves as borrowers shook their head affirmatively or negatively. This drama ended when the librarian touched the desired book and prisoners nodded "yes." This librarian also handled old donated legal books the same way, spending most of the work day walking to and from the back room to get material. Guarding the books instead of developing programs to enhance transformation. Other librarians used institutional security rules and protocols as rationale for not initiating or implementing programs, doing little more than providing popular reading, and the required reference materials. They did not hate their job. They just never used any initiative to engage the library users, majority of whom had never visited libraries prior to their incarceration. Observing this from the supervisory level made me understand the complaints from some prisoners when I worked at The Pen, and they got transferred to other institutions. Many of them wrote to me complaining about the shortcomings of the library services in their new location.

While not insurmountable, it was not easy to rectify this situation. Librarians in each institution across Maryland had very little opportunity to interact among one another since they were one-person managers providing services to all prisoners in their institutions. In each prison, the corrections education principal was the direct supervisor of librarians. The primary focus for many of these supervisors was GED. They were content with the librarian's presence, which reduced the grievances regarding lack of library access. Prisoners who never used libraries prior to incarceration were comfortable just having a quiet space to browse newspapers and magazines. These library users never complained about services unless they moved to or from other prisons where they had more positive experiences.

To create more engagement among the librarians, I set up meetings where they got together, shared experiences, ideas, and programs. Topics at these sessions included assessing users' needs, more effective use of electronic resources, reader's advisory, programs for soon-to-be-released prisoners to identify and create awareness of community resources, setting up displays, developing fliers that promote library services or programs, and training on software and technology. These meetings sometimes meant closing the libraries. Finding funds to hire substitute librarians. Paying for staff transport. Diverting funds from the well-needed collection, programs, and technology.

Telecommuting Librarian

Public perceptions of prisons being dangerous and unsafe resulted in very few qualified applicants for vacant positions in the prison libraries. The result was funds being transferred to other departments when a position remained vacant over a certain period. When I advertised for the position of a substitute librarian there was one qualified applicant. During the interview, this librarian expressed desire to work from home, saying there she could perform most of the duties outlined in the job requirement. I needed staff who would work directly in the prison and had no intention of hiring this applicant but my interest was sparked during our discussion, when she talked about her skills in web design. I felt that designing a website would be a definite plus to bridge the existing communication gap among the librarians. I felt that a tele-commuting librarian would have the time to research difficult questions and forward information to all the librarians, providing prisoners with more information than was presently possible. After the interview, to educate myself about schedules and details of the pros and cons of a telecommunicating librarian, I researched and visited libraries that used this service. I took the risk and hired this individual as a telecommuting librarian. The result was she developed a website for our library system, purchased all the required reference books, and researched many of the more difficult questions that the librarians did not have time to handle. Library staff were pleased with the outcomes from the work of our tele-commuting librarian and with our presentation, *The Kinks of a Telecom-muting Librarian*,[15] at the Maryland Library Association annual conferences.

Diversity

In 1987, when I was librarian at The Pen, the prison population was mostly African-Americans. In 1999, when I returned as library coordi-nator, the population was more diverse with more prisoners from Afri-can, Caribbean and Spanish-speaking countries. Mostly immigrants, these individuals informed me that they were not African-Americans. They wished to be identified and defined by their country of origin, e.g. Jamaicans, Africans, Mexicans, and were interested in materials from their own culture. Some of the Spanish-speaking prisoners were illiterate in their own language and were more interested in learning English. Sev-eral counties in Maryland and the Washington, D.C., area were having an influx of Spanish-speaking immigrants from South America. Job op-portunities for them were mostly as gardeners, house cleaners, nurse-maids, and cooks in restaurants. Others like MS-13 were in the drug trade. To educate myself for providing relevant services, I visited the Howard County Public Library system to examine their foreign language

---

[15] "Telecommuting for a Prison Library." http://olos.ala.org/columns/?p=98 https://olos.ala.org/columns/?p=94.

collection and used this as my guide to purchase materials with English as a second language and the few materials I could find in Spanish with trade information. When some of the African-American prisoners expressed the desire to learn Spanish so they could communicate with the Spanish-speaking population, I expanded the collection to include English and Spanish, purchasing mostly CD-ROMS after I realized that the printed versions of the dictionaries often disappeared from the library. Materials to accommodate diversity included large-print books, materials on transgender, gays, lesbian, close-captions materials for institutions with hearing-impaired prisoners, and books for the interest of the African and Caribbean population. Due to budget limitations, for the most part, the Maryland State Interlibrary Loan system became a great source, accommodating many requests for specific titles or subjects.

Reading Is Fundamental and Family Literacy

The vision of a reading program among prisoners and their children came to me the day I walked by the visiting area of a Jessup prison and saw the prisoners and their adult visitors talking and laughing with one another, while the children sat quietly beside them with very little or no engagement. I thought of ways to create positive interactions with these children. Placing children's books in the visiting areas was an option with setbacks. I had limited budget and books in this area may become media for hiding contraband items. Nevertheless, visualizing positive and educational outcomes from engagement among prisoners and children reading together, I shared the idea for a potential program with the MD Correctional Education Curriculum Specialist, Dr. Steve Steurer. We became partners in the organization of the program sponsored by Reading Is Fundamental (RIF), a nonprofit organization that provided books for disadvantaged children. We identified Jessup Correctional Institution (JCI), a medium-security prison, as the best choice for a successful outcome.

Approval and permission from the prison administration, as well as support from staff in the prison system, was crucial. One correctional education instructor became our key ally in communicating with the prison security staff. In the various meetings with **the warden and staff, I outlined the benefits of** prisoners reading with and to their children, pointing out that good reading skills, especially with parental involvement, would ultimately lead to educational and economic advancement and a reduction in juvenile incarceration. The emphasis during these conversations was that this engagement would also help the prisoners since a high percentage of them had poor reading skills or were illiterate. After weeks negotiating cost for additional security staff, criteria for participation among prisoners and outside guests, rules and protocols for interactions among the children, and visitors, we got permission to conduct the program.

Our next step was careful and intentional selection of prisoners who could be an inspiration and example for future groups. The instructor identified potential participants from among those with no history of institutional infractions or crimes against children, and who were willing to work with us as a team to plan and execute the program. We organized training and practice sessions that included prisoners reading the children's books purchased with RIF funds. Training meant prisoners had to learn and practice body and facial movements to keep the children engaged. Each time I saw the men using humor to hide their nervousness and discomfort, I would emphasize the importance of reading and the benefits for the children at the same time reminding and them of the necessity to adhere to DOC rules. After weeks of rehearsals, the men became more relaxed. Our first program went well. The prisoners said it was the most positive thing they had ever done with their children and as they became more confident and relaxed, they offered suggestions for future programs. Prison news spread about the program, resulting in a long waiting list of potential participants.[16] When we discontinued the relationship with RIF, the instructor renamed the program Reading Unites Family (RUF). After I retired from the system, the program continued with the dedication and support of the same instructor who worked with me at the beginning.

Family Literacy @ Your Library

Using the same Model as RIF and RUF, I initiated a similar program, *Family Literacy @ Your Library*, at the Maryland House of Corrections (MHC), a maximum-security prison. The nature of a maximum-security prison made negotiations and permissions more difficult. I invited the MHC librarian and a senior security staff at MHC to observe the RUF program. Impressed, they granted permission to implement Family Literacy, cautioning us to minimize outside publicity since a program like this could lead to negative public reactions about "benefits for criminals."

We identified potential leaders from among the prison population., circulated fliers to create awareness, and developed detailed training guidelines for the prisoners who would participate in the program. Fliers include words to draw interest:

> *Do you know children do better in school when family members encourage reading? Do you know that to do well in math, science, English, geography, or any other subject, a child must have reading skills developed to ease their struggle with*

---

[16] *Using Books to Maintain Family Ties in Maryland,* by Keith Martin, Asst. Editor, Corrections.com. 7/28/2003. http://www.corrections.com/articles/8986-using-books-to-maintain-family-ties-in-maryland.

words while trying to grapple with the meaning of the text?

Do you want to get involved with your children, grand-children, niece, nephew, or godchildren and help them im-prove in school?

If your answer is YES, speak to the MHC Librarian. We plan to develop activities that will help to stimulate your child's interest in learning.

The library clerks helped us identify prisoners whom they felt would be good fit for participating in the program and become Family Literacy Team Leaders. Our initial collection of children's books consisted of discards from public libraries. I gave these books to the team leaders, encouraging them to practice reading in their cells. I had no expertise in children's literature and programming, so I sought collaborative help from the head of the children's department at Enoch Pratt Free Library (EPFL). The children's librarian visited the prison, discussed reading techniques, and practiced reading children's book with the men. During their first rehearsals, she had the prisoners practicing the Hokey Pokey song and various moves to keep the children engaged. As I watched the willingness of the men attempting to do the Hokey Pokey moves, I was happy that they still wanted to participate in the program despite their obvious discomfort. I tried to keep a straight face so as not to increase their discomfort when I saw them trying to copy the Hokey Pokey moves of the female librarian. EPFL lent us a basic collection of children's books. We cordoned off an area with the sign "FAMILY LITERACY." During one visit to MHC, I noticed that some prisoners selected books from this section, then moved far away from the area to read the books. I understood by then that they may be embarrassed to be seen in an area reading children's books. I adjusted the sign to *"Family Literacy. Books you can read with and to your children."* This made a difference. Many readers remained in the Family Literacy section after this sign was posted.

I applied for and received grants from Citizens for Maryland Libraries (CML)[17] and the Barbara Bush Foundation,[18] These funds became the startup children's collection for some prison libraries in Maryland.

Each time Family Literacy team leaders said they had never seen these children's titles, nor read to their children, I reminded them that although it may be difficult, they should try to put aside the tough macho image and practice reading so they would feel comfortable with the children who would be attending.

"I'm sure you don't want these children to think you cannot read since it may mean they focus more on your discomfort rather than listen to what you are reading," I said.

The Saturday morning of the first event, the MHC librarian and I arrived early. We looked around the visiting room admiring the beautiful decorations and pictures created and set up by the prisoners. We waited in anticipation of the children's arrival. The literacy team and the prisoners who got permission to participate came and sat in the visiting room, waiting. That first day, only one little boy came with his grandmother. Though disappointed, I decided to proceed with the program as planned. I told the men that this was an opportunity for them to participate by playing in the role of children. The team member who volunteered to read was a young man who was not a father. As he began reading to the little boy and the other prisoners, I noticed that his hands were shaking and heard a tremor in his voice, signaling nervousness.

Seated beside the child, I said, "You know, Sam, this is the first time that Mr. Dee is reading to children, so he may be a little nervous, but we are going to listen and help him, right?"

---

[17] https://www.citizensformarylandlibraries.org/.
[18] https://en.wikipedia.org/wiki/Barbara_Bush_Foundation_for_Family_Literacy.

Dee continued reading just as we had rehearsed. At the end of the program, he thanked me for helping out because my intervention made him more relaxed. Dee became very involved in the Family Literacy and other programs in the prison system. When he was transferred to another prison across the state, he asked me to start a program in that region. Majority of the prisoners and their families lived in Baltimore, so transport to these faraway prisons would be a problem and some residents in that institution said they even had difficulty getting to the library for regular use. I did not set up a Family Literacy program there.

I lost touch with Dee over the years. When I decided to retire, I visited all the prison libraries to say farewell. I saw and greeted Dee informing him it was my last prison visit as I would be retiring. He looked shocked, then said he appreciated all the work I did. As I was leaving the visiting area he came toward me.

"I know I may get in trouble for touching you, Ms. Shirley, but as you are leaving, and I may not see you again, I am going to give you a hug," he said.

He hugged me in clear view of the officers. Moved by his gesture, I exited the room quickly before my tearful emotions took over. Years later, a prison advocate who was working to get Dee on parole told me that Dee shared with her that the day I walked out so quickly after his hug, he thought my speedy exit was due to my being offended by a hug from a prisoner. Later, when he read an article about my retirement in *The Washington Post*, he realized that it was emotion, not annoyance, that made me exit with such haste.

The success of the Family Literacy program resulted in a long waiting list. I modified the program, allowing each parent and child to participate for three sessions, enabling others to get an opportunity. Listening to and observing the interactions among the participants, I decided to incorporate topics on parenting, challenges in schools, teenage issues, and quizzes to keep the children engaged. In the beginning, the warden and staff said participating children could be no older than 8 years old. However, as discussions became a part of the program, many prisoners said they had older children who were at an age where they needed to have discussions with an adult male that they never thought about until they got involved with the Family Literacy Program. I shared their comments with the warden and his security staff, pointing out that many of the children of prisoners end up in the juvenile system. They came and observed several of our programs. I also involved security staff by asking them to hand out certificates to participating children. After these events, I got approval to include older children, again with the caution, "We don't want the public to start complaining about how these prisoners have the luxury of their children coming in to read together, instead of being punished for the crimes they commit."

I understood the validity of their concern since I too have been the recipient of similar comments from individuals who said prisoners should be punished, not rewarded.

My response to these comments was: "Majority of the incarcerated individuals eventually leave prison and go back into the society. It makes more social and economic sense to educate them so when they return to society, they adjust better socially and this also will help them to get a job on the outside and become taxpayers. That way, my tax dollars can be used to provide more children with a better education and enable them to be more productive in the society. "

Validating moments for me were prisoners' comments. After one program, a prisoner looking pleased and, with awe in his voice, said, "I never know my child could read."

Another said, "It couldn't get any righter than this."

Reading through Community Collaborations

When the prisoners and their family members said they never visited their local public libraries, I again collaborated with EPFL. The staff gave me library membership cards, forms, and prizes for children to participate in the library's summer reading games. I advertised and distributed these to the visitors and prisoners during the reading sessions, encouraging the prisoners to mail them to family members.

FAMILY LITERACY @ YOUR LIBRARY- MHC

SUMMER READING GAME

PLEASE REMEMBER TO HAVE YOUR CHILD READ AND FILL OUT THE SUMMER READING SHEET.

THE CHILD WILL GET PRIZES BASED ON THE NUMBER OF BOOKS READ.

***YOU** **DO NOT WANT YOUR CHILD TO FEEL LEFT OUT WHEN** WE ARE GIVING OUT THE PRIZES ON JULY 23.*

CALL THEM, REMIND THEM TO READ AND FILL OUT THE FORMS. CAREGIVERS MAY READ WITH A SMALL CHILD.

SEND THE FORMS BEFORE JULY 23, THE CHILD

GETS THE PRIZES ON JULY 23.

Additional prizes for those reading over 10 books

We initiated the summer reading games in the prison library, distributing the same shirts that participants on the outside got from their respective libraries. Prisoners were pleased. Their evaluation comments were testament.

Now I can be silly with my child. Before this I never knew I could do that.

I'm 44 years old and I can now relate better with my girlfriend's children.

I have learned so much about reading to children.

A visiting grandmother said, *"This is first time my son admits to his daughter that he is in prison. When she visited him before, she used to wonder why she could not spend the night at Daddy's house."*

Developing a CD-ROM

It was the age of the internet. Security concerns prohibited prisoners from having direct access to this technology. Realizing the great disadvantage for the incarcerated men when they returned to their communities, I made a commitment to do something, anything, to correct this. Technology was not my strong point but I knew that anything I did to enhance knowledge would be helpful. Each evening in the quiet of my home, I put myself in the place of an incarcerated individual who had absolutely no knowledge of the internet. Starting at the very base, I developed a script: "What is a mouse? How to use a mouse to navigate the computer. What is a web address? How to search online for different topics, type in a website address, navigate a page, search for a library in a community, topics on health, community resources, write a resume, apply for a job online, and how to print a document."

I realized that it would be more effective to have detailed audio instructions on how to use this technology resource, and sought the help of a public speaker to do the narration, investigated companies to produce the final product at a reasonable price. Baltimore County Public Library's (BCPL) technology department produced the CD-ROM at a rate significantly lower than the private companies. The BCPL technology staff were very patient working with me on several mock samples as I made adjustments based on awareness of the prisoners' backgrounds, literacy skills, and education levels. After several months of testing and retesting, the final product was ready. Contents on the CD-ROM captured and promoted many sites from the homepages of the libraries in the two communities that were home to most of the prisoners—Enoch Pratt and the Prince George County Memorial Libraries. The sites listed community resources for the men to seek information when they returned to society as the narrator's voice guided users to specific internet sites for employment, housing, career opportunities, GED, and to Maryland's CareerNet Centers.

To garner support and get permission from the DOC administration, I requested an opportunity to demonstrate the CD-ROM at one of their executive meeting. They liked the educational aspect of the CD-ROM, gave approval for implementation in all the prison libraries and later rewarded me with a certificate of recognition for developing "Discovering the Internet @ Your Library."

Each of the Maryland prison libraries received a CD-ROM. Librarians and library clerks received training on how to use the product that they would eventually make available to the general prison population. During that period, Maryland prison libraries were the only prison libraries in the United States to have this kind of CD-ROM. To create national awareness, I did presentations at the annual conferences of the Correctional Education Association and the American Library Association. This resulted in requests for copies of the CD-ROM from prison librarians and transition specialists across the country. When I received a request for a copy of this CD-ROM from a prison librarian in a South American Spanish-speaking country, I negotiated sending a free copy in return for a Spanish translation of the CD-ROM. This enabled equal access for the increasing number of Spanish-speaking prisoners.

Chapter 8
Community Collaboration and Reentry

When they leave prison, formerly incarcerated individuals encounter many barriers. They return to families and environments in the same neighborhoods they lived prior to incarceration. For the most part, their hometowns had little or no job opportunities and the same negative surroundings they left before going to prison. With little or no work history, they have to deal with public perception of them being illiterate, violent, and possessing incurable habits. The ultimate results include fear, distrust, and low expectations on all sides. Job attainment being almost impossible, many formerly incarcerated individuals said that their only option was to return to pre-conviction activities. This resulted in a high rate of reincarceration. With a goal to create more positive interactions, trust, and to lessen fear and distrust among prisoners and members of the community, I initiated some community collaborations.

The One Maryland One Book, sponsored by the Maryland Humanities, and Read Across America, were organizations that provided opportunities for free books, book discussions, and visits from outside guests. Each year, Maryland Humanities donated books to the Maryland prison libraries enabling the library users to participate in book discussions. On one occasion Maryland Humanities adjusted their statewide schedule so that Warren St. John, author of *Outcast United*, could visit the Jessup Correctional Institute (JCI). Before the author's visit a few prisoners requested another book that the author had written. I used my personal public library card to borrow this title, sought and got permission from prison administration to take this book into the institution. The men expressed appreciation that I made the effort to get this book.

The day the author visited, the men listened, made comments, and asked many questions during the discussion period. One prisoner said he migrated from Africa and identified fully with the football players described in the book. Another said the way the outcasts from different areas bonded together as football players was similar to their situation in the prison when they got together in the recreation yard for various games. The author was surprised when one of the men asked him about the difference in the writing in two of his books. The conversation would have continued, but it was time for the men to return to their cells. St. John said that in his book tour travels across the country, this location was one of his most engaging.

I invited outside guests like authors, staff from EPFL, writers, motivational speakers, college students, and college interns, knowing that this engagement enabled prisoners to develop some comfort and more trust in libraries and individuals outside the prison walls. This interaction also provided the visitors with opportunities to see prisoners as human beings rather than thinking of or fearing them because of their criminal convictions.

Library Snapshot Day

When The American Library Association initiated Library Snapshot Day, where libraries across the country took random photographs of user activities to demonstrate the value of libraries, I also took random photos from three prisons to show the various activities occurring in Maryland prison libraries. This also brought some understanding and awareness to persons on the outside.

Reentry

When Cal left prison, his wife sent a letter to friends and supporters on the outside. The letter included details of his reentry into society, increasing my awareness of the many obstacles that confront formerly incarcerated individuals. Majority of the Maryland's prisoners are from east side of Baltimore city, primarily in the areas surrounding Johns Hopkins Hospital medical campus. Except for moving from prison to prison in various counties in Maryland, these individuals rarely moved outside their area of birth. The result was, and still is, when they leave the prison, their only option is to return to their old neighborhood of mostly crime, drugs, drug users, dealers, and unemployed friends who hang out on the streets. They become part of the Bureau of Justice statistics, a recidivism rate of over 67.8% recidivism within three years.[19]

Reentry to society is very difficult, especially for prisoners who were confined for long periods. Many of them return to a domestic environment very different from the one they experienced in prison, where every movement was organized, they had free access to roof over their head, a bed, clothes, and meals, and various means of entertainment. Adjusting in the outside world without significant preparation was therefore difficult. Some of the obstacles they encounter include lack of funds for housing and other basic needs. Inadequate knowledge and access to healthcare services, especially mental health situations and drug rehabilitation centers. Family conflicts. Inability to get a job due

---

[19] Bureau of Justice. Recidivism. http://www.bjs.gov/index.cfm?ty=tp&tid=17#pubs.

in some cases to lack of education, work-related skills, work history, and hiring discrimination based on their criminal records, and race. During their incarceration many prisoners earn their GED, get a university degree, and learn various skills. This placed them on a higher level in the prison system, where they were the ones who were in charge of the organizations they got approval to set up in the prison. These accomplishments for the most part do not help them in their need to adjust, or secure employment if they do not get community and political support.

Family Relations

The domestic situation facing the returning resident who has been incarcerated for long periods is an area of reentry that is often overlooked. Prior to incarceration, the money they accumulated from their illegal activities made many of these men the major breadwinners and THE MAN in the house and among family members. This gained them respect, and control over their family and friends. During incarceration the women, grandmothers, mothers, sisters, aunts, girlfriends become the primary decision makers, heads of households, sole income earners, and single parents. The children, with no father around, depend on and take orders from these women. Most noteworthy, although women are still underpaid compared with the men, and many experienced racial inequities, some became beneficiaries under the equal opportunity laws, and were employed in jobs from which they were previously excluded.

The expectation of many of the men when they return to their communities is to resume their pre-prison status and be acknowledged as THE MAN around the house. They have great difficulty in and refuse to accept the changed domestic situation, resulting in domestic violence and leading to reincarceration.

In the prison environment, emphasis is often more on legal information services for long-term prisoners to reduce the grievances and lawsuits regarding their right of access to courts. Aware that lack of reentry
information contributed to the high reincarceration rate, I contacted
public libraries and got their discarded versions of books of all kinds but
especially materials on jobs, community resources, services, and library
brochures about public library programs that would be relevant to reentry needs. I also invited pubic librarians to give talks to the soon-to-be-
released prisoners in order to educate them about public libraries in their
communities. At one event, towards the end of the librarian's presentation, a prisoner asked about the cost to get the materials from the public
library. He was surprised when the librarian told him that there was no
cost for borrowing a book or getting services from the public library.

Prison Bookmobile

Driving through one of the Baltimore neighborhoods one day, I saw
an Enoch Pratt Free Library bookmobile parked alongside the road. It
reminded me of my bookmobile experience in Jamaica and in the
United States so I parked, went onto the unit, and questioned the library staff about the neighborhoods they visited and the customers they
served. The librarian's response made me think of the positive and effective outcomes of a bookmobile with relevant reentry materials and
programs for prisoners at prerelease centers. It would be a great educational and transforming experience for these prisoners. I followed up
this idea by visiting several libraries that provided bookmobile services,
gathered information on the kinds of services they provided, the companies that sold the vehicle, and other pertinent information.

With the data I collected and the active support of the organization's transition coordinator, I requested a meeting with senior staff at

the correctional administrative headquarters, presenting them with information on the benefits of relevant information, materials, and technology for pre-released prisoners, from a mobile unit going to various prerelease centers across the state. I informed them that bookmobile services, programs, and contents would enable soon-to-be-released prisoners access to knowledge and job skills through library education, enabling a more successful community reintegration. I said that since majority of the prisoners said they never visited libraries outside of prisons, we would provide them with information that would make them more willing to visit their libraries to get more information on community resources during their transition.

After several meetings and discussions including protocols, I got permission to purchase a bookmobile using inmate welfare funds (money accumulated from charging prisoners for telephone services and commissary items). I researched companies, sought and got assistance from one of the correctional education instructors who did motor racing and owned a large vehicle that he used to transport his racing vehicles to the various states. He was very helpful in guiding me and contacting the companies, informing them of the technology I wanted on the bookmobile. I purchased two bookmobiles, for the Maryland Western and the Eastern regions. These bookmobiles were the only ones in the prison system across the United States in 2007. In 2010, online university blog listed Maryland Prison libraries as one of ten U.S. Prisons with Impressive Libraries.[20]

At the American Library Association Conference in Washington, D.C., in 2007, our bookmobile was one of the vehicles on display. A young man saw the unit with the prison sign and, out of curiosity, came up to the door. I invited him inside. The librarians and I had a long conversation with him. He told us that he had been incarcerated in several

---

[20] https://www.onlineuniversities.com/blog/2010/12/10-u-s-prisons-with-impressive-libraries/.

states, but the prison libraries helped him to be a better person. He said he came up to the bookmobile because he saw the word "prison" and was curious. As he departed, he thanked the librarians, saying that even if our effort impacted only one person, it was a good thing. [21]

The mobile collections included books on various trades, how to set up businesses, apply for jobs, doing interviews, family relations, getting advanced education like GED or college degrees, writing resumes and cover letters, licensing information, employment possibilities, restoring credit, locations for housing agencies and homeless shelters, substance abuse, health and career centers, ESL materials. With the help of technology experts in the correctional educational system, we added computers with internet access. The goal was to have staff conduct sessions on how to search the internet for jobs and fill out application forms online. Our fliers included job positions from various areas, sample reference questions, and public library fliers from various regions.

One poignant bookmobile moment for me was seeing a prisoner enter the bookmobile in handcuffs. I thought that the security staff would remove these handcuffs but they did not. The handcuffed prisoner sat at the computer desk in the van as he tried to follow our instructions, his cuffed hands moving slowly across the computer keyboard. He thanked us for coming to the prison.

Bookmobile Questions from Prisoners

- *Do you have a list of transitional houses in Prince George County?*
- *I need the address of the Baltimore City District Court.*
- *What is needed in order to obtain a certification as an addiction counselor?*

---

[21] Bookmobile on Parade. http://olos.ala.org/columns/?p=91.

- *Are there any apprenticeship programs in masonry in Baltimore?*
- *How do I go about starting my own clothing store?*
- *How do I start a garbage collecting business?*
- *How do I apply for a Maryland I.D. card?*
- *I'd like to be a foster parent and I live in Washington, D.C. Do you have info about that?*
- *Can ex-offenders obtain a U.S. passport, and if so how do I go about it?*
- *Do you have information on disability housing in Baltimore City?*
- *I need the address of the Maryland State Board of Cosmetologists. I need to renew my license.*
- *Are there job openings for cooks in Dundalk?*
- *I need information on bonding.*
- *What is an Alford Plea?*

Reentry Conversations

Man around the House

Many incarcerated females said they were in prison because their boyfriends or husbands forced them into drugs and prostitution. Others said they killed, shot, or stabbed their male partners, in retaliation against violent and abusive behaviors. To create some awareness of women's progress and accomplishments, I organized a program designed to educate the men who were working very hard to leave prison. My goal was to help them understand some of the domestic changes they may encounter since many of them were reincarcerated because of domestic violence.

Women's History Month, I invited guest speakers to the Jessup Correctional Institution (JCI male institution) to discuss women's equal right issues, laws, civil rights, work environment, etc. The guest panel included a religious volunteer who helped women in poor communities, a male social worker on community services, and a speaker giving details about voting, civil rights, equal rights, historic events, initiatives, and accomplishment of women. The post-event discussion was lively and positive with full participation among the prisoners until one of the younger prisoners asked to speak.

"I know we in here," he said, "and the women have to take care of business while we in here. But when we go back home them should step aside and let us wear the pants and be the man."

"You have to remember that during a prisoner's incarceration the women are often the sole breadwinners, and make major decisions on almost everything. They were often the only ones available to the children as well. That means it may not be easy or fair to ask them to just step back, even though they may still be the main breadwinner, especially since it is difficult for formerly incarcerated persons to get jobs," I said.

"You saying that we must start wear skirts then?" he asked.

"If you are comfortable doing that, it would really be up to you," I said, directing my gaze to another prisoner who had a question. I did not want his comment to be the focus for the very brief period the prisoners had left before they returned to their cells.

After the session, I overheard several of the older prisoners chastising him for his attitude. I did not stay around to listen as I had to escort the guests outside the prison gates.

Employment and the Need for Money

Patuxent Institution, the only one of its kind in Maryland, was established to handle the most dangerous criminal offenders through psychotherapeutic treatment. Staff consisted primarily of clinicians, social workers, psychologists, and psychiatrists, with emphasis on treatment.

Many incarcerated men in the various Maryland prisons used the library to get information on how to qualify for entry into Patuxent. They said that the variety of programs at Patuxent provided them with a better chance to exit the prison system earlier.

On one of my visits to Patuxent, a prisoner came up to me and said hello. He said that he recognized me from one of the other prisons. I inquired whether his stay at Patuxent was due to transfer from another prison. He said no, he had been released, went home for a while, but now was back in prison.

"You come to the library to seek information to leave prison, then when you go home you end up right back here. Why did you even bother to try to leave?" I asked.

"You know, Ms. Shirley, I learned a trade in prison. When I got home I need $500 to get my license, but I had no one to lend me. I went to my friends. Most of them were still on the street selling dope, and they just say to me, 'Man, you know how and where you can get the money.' And it was not even that activity that bring me back here, you know, Ms. Shirley, is a longtime charge that the police had on me when they stop me in an area they usually patrol."

You Helped Me

It was the end of my workday. I left my office on Baltimore Street, heading for the parking garage on Fayette. I stood at the corner waiting for the traffic to ease so I could cross the road. Heading towards the garage entrance, I made eye contact with a youngish-looking male who said, "Hello, Ms., you used to work in the prison over there?" He pointed eastward, where Maryland Penitentiary and several other prisons are located. I looked into a face I did not recognize, hesitating a few seconds before answering in the affirmative.

"You used to help me find books to read, and now I am working."

"Great," I said. "Now I hope you are keeping out of trouble, for if not, it means that the books I got for you did not help."

He sat on the side of the road and, with a laugh, said, "I have a job now, and I am keeping straight. I really appreciate your help."

"Have a good day," I said, "and don't let me down."

He laughed again.

I moved forward, waiting by the garage entrance until he moved on in the opposite direction. I did not remember anything about this individual, but felt good that he benefitted from library services in the prison.

Second Chance

From an aisle in a Columbia, MD, store, I moved aside as a young man passed. He looked at me, then stopped.

"Hi," he said.

I smiled and continued to look at the shelves, expecting him to continue up the aisle.

Instead he asked, "I remember you. You the lady who used to work at the jail?"

Ugh, ugh, I thought as I smiled at him and nodded my head in affirmation.

"That book, *Second Chance,* that you lent me was really helpful. Is like they were talking about my life. I'm going straight now. Thank you again."

"Good luck," I said.

Conclusion

As the librarian first providing direct services to prisoners, then later as coordinator responsible for all the state prison libraries, I learned many lessons mostly from discussions with the prison library users. As human beings most of us are comfortable staying physically and mentally within our own racial, socioeconomic, and intellectual groups. We often use the passage of the Civil Rights Act as evidence that discrimination ended, justifying our blaming and judging mostly persons of color who are unable to find jobs to move out of their impoverished and high-crime communities. We condemn individuals who see the drug trade as their only sources of income. The irony, as some prisoners pointed out to me, is that the real criminals were the invisible owners of the boats, airplanes, and luxury cars who took the drugs to the various neighborhoods, setting up the drug trade as a business. These invisible individuals were also the ones who really made big money, but never got caught, especially since many of them were often financial supporters and friends of politicians.

My daily interactions with these men and women, outcasts in our society, made me realize that all they need is encouragement, education, being recognized as individuals regardless of their race, and to be given an opportunity to pay back or start over in a more positive and supportive environment.

My hope is that our country does not revel in our world ranking as number one in incarceration and number 27 in education and healthcare, justifying the high rate of incarceration as being "tough on crime." Taxpayers like myself are the ones who pay for the high cost of incarceration. To those who are employed in the penal system and who keep telling me that they would not have a job if there were no prisons or prisoners, I often respond, "If we have positive and supportive infrastructures, the jobs for majority of you would be as security staff, social worker, or counsellors within the school systems or other intentionally constructed educational and social environments. These would be supportive areas that help underprivileged and underserved citizens towards more positive and uplifting opportunities and careers. Think of the great mentors and guides you would be for students and at-risk youths," I said to one corrections officer.

Our country will do better and become great if we spend more of our money on education than incarceration, putting in place infrastructures that will give the underclass hope, encouragement, inspiration, and aspirations.

Most importantly, we must address the overt racism in a society where a police officer felt justified in arresting an African-American juvenile, while sending his white companion home in a situation where both of them were doing the same thing together. This action was so openly egregious that the white boy challenged the officer, saying it was not right because they were both guilty of the same thing.

The contents of majority of the prisoners' correspondences with me made me feel that my interactions with them in the library provided positive influence and gave them hope.

One prisoner's comment about his library experience confirmed this. "You feel like you are not in a prison anymore. No bars in here."

Another prisoner's comment after a book discussion: "I really love the book discussions we have in the prison library. You see, when we were on the street we have to show off that we were tough men. We don't show our feelings. In here we read this book and find the character in the book has the same issues we have. It takes a little while, but after a time the brothers in the book discussion group begin to open up. Nobody is judging you and we feel a little freer to explore our feelings since more or less we all share the same experience."

RQ's letter on a sheet of paper folded into a card with the handwritten words were my encouragement to continue to be a library advocate in and out of prison.

Glennor Shirley

To: G-Nora S. Best of luck for the Holidays

Love of Words

Let there be light and it was,
The brightness of Love and life are in words,
The skin and Body holds Fast to the command of it,
As you place yourself around it and become part of it.
It's a wonder and a good thing to know,
Why you chose to become a Librarian
The power of life is in words and
All is possible in it, and through IT
{Written through the Inspiration of knowing you)

Bookmobile Maryland Prison Library

Bookmobile internet instruction

Library Users

Reentry books on prison bookmobile

Preparing for Reentry

Prison Library Users

Summer Reading at Your Prison Library

Supervising Prison Literacy

Women's Prison Library

CPSIA information can be obtained
at www.ICGtesting.com
Printed in the USA
LVHW072243090720
660290LV00013B/1780

* 9 7 8 1 6 4 7 0 2 2 2 0 4 *